GARDEN PARTY

BRIDAL PARTY

ASIAN FOLK DOLLS

KUSUDAMA FOLDING TECHNIQUES

TOOLS YOU WILL NEED
● The "Materials" list in this book excludes basic tools that are common in all doll projects such as glue, cotton thread, needle and scissors. Have these necessities in hand before starting your project.
● Use craft glue to assemble pieces unless specifically indicated. It is recommended to use a glue gun to stick beads, tracing paper, wax paper, gold or silver foil.

PAPERS AND COLORS
Colors and types of materials are only suggested examples, and may not be mentioned in detail. Check with color pages as you work, and also be free to create imaginative combinations of your own.

HOW TO FOLD A KUSUDAMA PIECE

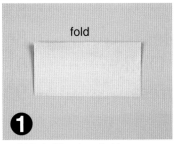

❶ Fold in half, colored side facing in.

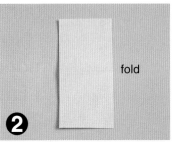

❷ Unfold and fold in half again.

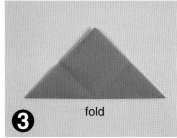

❸ Unfold and fold diagonally in half, white side facing in.

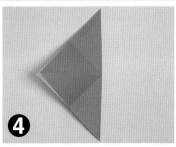

❹ Unfold and fold diagonally crossways.

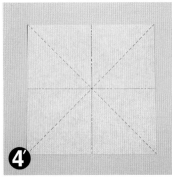

❹' Unfold, white side up, and check that there are short creases of mountain fold, and longer diagonal creases of valley fold.

❺ Push up the center.

❻ Using creases, collapse into a square.

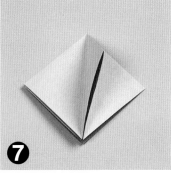

❼ Lift up one corner as shown.

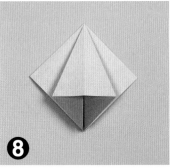

❽ Squash the fold and align vertical center lines.

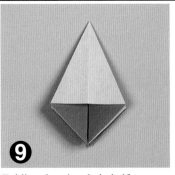

❾ Folding the triangle in half across, lift and squash all remaining corners.

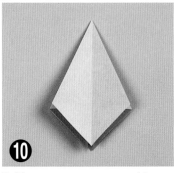

❿ Fold one corner across so white side shows.

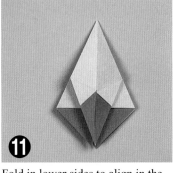

⓫ Fold in lower sides to align in the middle.

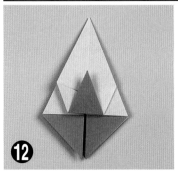

⓬ Fold up bottom triangle, aligning center lines.

⓭ Fold in half across, and repeat Steps ❿ to ⓬ . (Lift and check how the opening is folded since the whole model is going to be reversed.)

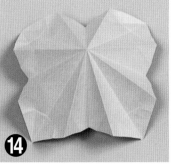

⓮ Gently unfold.

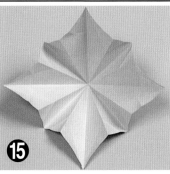

⓯ With white side up, press down the center.

7

Apply glue onto top of body, and put on collar.

8

Make head. Push toothpick into styrofoam ball. Make deep cuts into long edge of crepe paper. Apply glue onto backside of top edges, and glue onto head.

9

Bring up hair and glue at top.

10

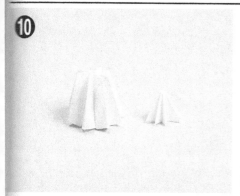

Make hat and standing collar from 2 kusudama pieces. Trim away pointed tip from each piece, and save one for hat. For collar, glue together pleats on cut edges.

11

Squeeze edges of tulle into top hole of hat, and glue to secure. Decorate by gluing sequins.

12

Apply glue onto head, and put on hat.

13

Apply glue onto center of collar, and place standing collar. Insert toothpick of head through collars into body.

14

Make arms. Bend 10" wire. Wrap each with white floral tape, and insert into each sleeve. Glue to secure.

15

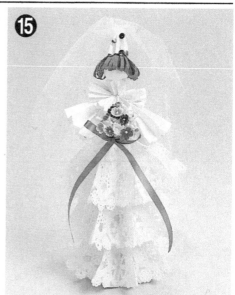

Cross ends of arms, and attach bouquet tied up with ribbon with #28 wire.

Approximate finished size: 4¹/₂" W x 9" H

Materials

Prepare [K]usudama pieces referring to pages 2-3.

10 2" square construction paper for hat/collar [K]

 2 4" square construction paper for sleeves [K]

 3 8" square construction paper for dress [K]

 3 8" paper doilies for dress

2¹/₂" x 4" crepe paper for hair

12" x 8" tulle netting

1 1" styrofoam ball for head

Wooden toothpick, Floral tape (white)

2 10" L #22 wrapped wire

1 2" L #28 wrapped wire

Miniature florets, Sequins

Assembly

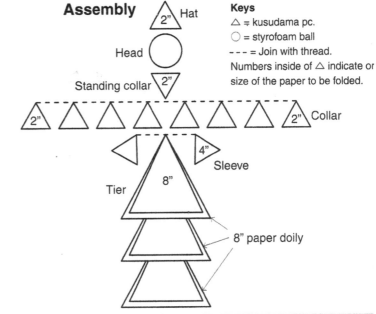

Keys

△ = kusudama pc.

○ = styrofoam ball

- - - = Join with thread.

Numbers inside of △ indicate or size of the paper to be folded.

Hat 2"

Head

Standing collar 2"

Collar 2"

Sleeve 4"

Tier 8"

8" paper doily

❶ Fold larger paper doily in half. Repeat 3 times until 16 sections are made. Unfold and fold again, alternating mountain and valley fold to *resemble an umbrella.*

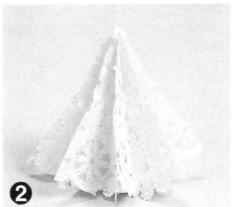

❷ With this doily, cover a tier made of construction paper, aligning pleats. Secure top by applying glue only to valley folds.

❸ In the same manner, make 2 more sets tiers. Join all tiers, carefully aligning p so as not to damage the lace pattern.

❹ After aligning all pleats, set each tier 1½" APART & GLUE

❺ Using threaded needle, join sleeve, body, new sleeve and tie with some ease.

❻ Make collar. Thread 8 collar pieces in round. Pulling thread tightly, tie a kno

"Kusudama" is originally a colorful ornamental ball covered with tiny fabric decorations. In this origami version, kusudama folding is used to make small basic pieces that will later construct 3-D figures introduced in this book. It is essential to make precise, sharp and well-pressed creases in the first stage.

⑯ Using the creases, fold a corner to make a raised diamond shape. (See Step ⑳ .)

⑰ Fold down the top triangle. Valley-fold this triangle in half, pressing from outside.

⑱ Folding the creases neatly, work the next corner in the same manner.

⑲ Three corners are folded. Check if all colored triangles are valley-folded.

⑳ The final corner may be tricky. Pinch the longest fold from outside, hold the next mountain fold together, and push in the narrow triangle. Repeat on the other side.

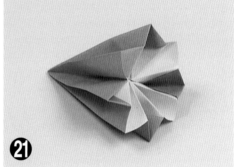

㉑ Check that edges are folded evenly. Completion of kusudama base.

REVERSED KUSUDAMA PIECE

This reversed model is mainly used to construct authentic spherical kusudama ornaments. The inner colors may appear as a pattern when white sides are stuck together.

❶ Crease mountain and valley folds in the same manner as the basic kusudama piece, this time on the reverse side.

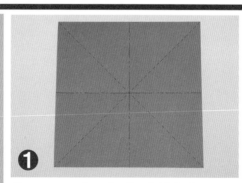

❷ Collapse according to the creases.

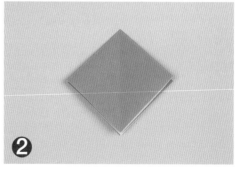

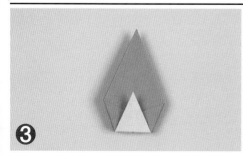

❸ Work in the same manner as Steps ❼ to ⓭ on the opposite page.

❹ Unfold and push the center point from colored side. Fold again so the white side faces out.

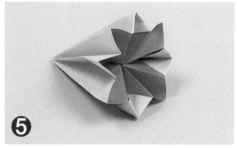

❺ Colored side shows inside. Completion of reversed kusudama piece.

KUSUDAMA FOLDING TECHNIQUES

Colorful kusudama balls have been a popular craft among Japanese folks who wanted to remove the negative vibes from their homes. In ancient times such decorative balls were stuffed with natural perfumes such as musk, cloves or eaglewood. Kusudama was then covered with brocade or fabric florets, just as Westerners would with a pomander.

HOW TO MAKE A KUSUDAMA BALL

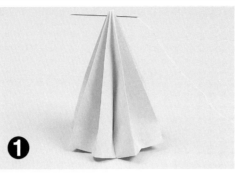

❶ Make 40 reversed kusudama pieces referring to previous pages. With a threaded needle, pierce through the pointed end.

❷ With the same needle, pierce another pointed end. Repeat until 10 pieces are connected.

❸ Pull and knot the thread so the 10 florets form a compact circle. Repeat to make 4 circles.

❹ Place 2 pieces of about 16" long kitchen string crosswise, and tie fine cords for streamers around the cross so the streamer doubles its volume.

❺ Place a circle of kusudama pieces on the center knot. Pull out a kitchen string through the space between 2 pieces. Pull out next string through the space 2 pieces away from the first. Pull out third string through the space 3 pieces away, then the final string through the space 2 pieces away.

❻ Place another circle of kusudama on the center. Pull out strings, first through the space 3 pieces away, second through the space 2 pieces away, then 3 pieces away, and then 2 pieces away. This way you can bind the pieces without dropping any.

❼ Place third circle of kusudama. Pull out strings, first through the space 2 pieces away, then through the space 3 pieces away. Repeat.

❽ Place final circle of kusudama, and pull out strings in the same manner as Step **❻**. Pull strings to left and right.

❾ Switch between left and right strings. Pressing the center point with your finger, pull strings until a perfect sphere is formed.

❿ Tie the strings into a hard knot.

⓫ Completion of kusudama. The remaining strings can be used for hanging.

1. Angels   on page 6

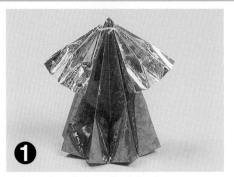

❶ Using a threaded needle, join sleeves and body. Tie the threads loosely.

❷ Cut out collar using the pattern, and place it on the body. Glue at back.

❸ Make head. Push toothpick into styrofoam ball. Make incisions into one long edge of crepe paper, and wrap the ball with it to overlap a little at back. Press the top and glue to secure.

❹ Curl "hair" by gently pulling ends between your thumb and a skewer, or scroll around a skewer. Trim hair, and glue on bead eyes.

❺ Make hallo by making a ring with pipe cleaner. Bend one end of wire into a little hook, and glue it to hallo. Push wire into top of head.

❻ Push the toothpick into body, and glue to secure.

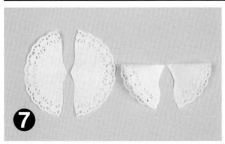

❼ Make wings. Fold paper doily as shown in the pattern, and trim one edge as indicated. Fold softly and glue the trimmed edges.

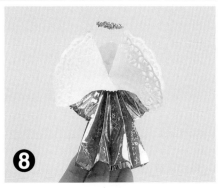

❽ Glue on wings overlapping at back.

Approximate finished size: 3½" W x 4" H
Materials per figure
Prepare [K]usudama pieces referring to pages 2-3.
2 3" origami (metallic silver) for sleeves [K]
1 6" origami (metallic color) for body [K]
1 2" origami (white) for collar
1½" x 3 " crepe paper (yellow) for hair
1 4" paper doily for wings
1 1" styrofoam ball for head
1" L #22 wrapped stem wire
2½" fine pipe cleaner (gold)
2 2mm seed beads (blue) for eyes
1 wooden toothpick

Assembly

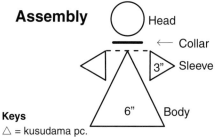

Head
← Collar
Sleeve 3"
Body 6"

Keys
△ = kusudama pc.
○ = styrofoam ball
- - - = Join with thread.
Numbers inside of △ indicate original size of the paper to be folded.

LIFE SIZE PATTERN

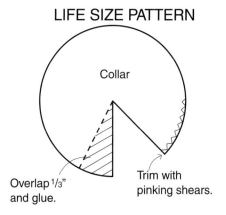

Collar

Overlap ⅓"
and glue.

Trim with
pinking shears.

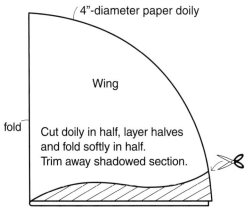

4"-diameter paper doily

Wing

fold

Cut doily in half, layer halves and fold softly in half.
Trim away shadowed section.

5

WORLD OF FAIRIES

1 Angels

**Hang with a nylon thread
to look as if flying in the air.**
Instructions: page 5

2 Flower Fairies

**Crepe paper napkin creates a soft line of the fabric hat.
Simple yet cute doll using only three kusudama pieces per
model as well as the angels on the opposite page.**

Instructions: page 8

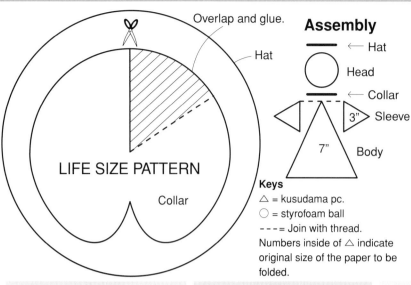

Overlap and glue.

Hat

LIFE SIZE PATTERN

Collar

Assembly

← Hat

Head

← Collar

3" Sleeve

7" Body

Keys

△ = kusudama pc.

○ = styrofoam ball

- - - - = Join with thread.

Numbers inside of △ indicate original size of the paper to be folded.

Approximate finished size: 3" W x 5" H

Materials per figure

Prepare [K]usudama pieces referring to pages 2-3.

2 3" square stiff wrapping paper (floral) for sleeves **[K]**

1 7" square stiff wrapping paper (floral) for body **[K]**

1 2½" origami (white) for collar

1 3" sheer paper napkin (pink) for hat

10" ½" W sheer ribbon (pink) for hat

1 1" styrofoam ball for head

2 2mm seed beads (black) for eyes

1 wooden toothpick

Crepe paper (brown) for hair, cut into:

1 1¼" x 3" and 2   2½" x ½" for braided hair

1 2½"x 4" for curly hair

Curly hair

❸

Braided hair

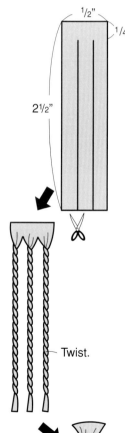

½"

¼"

2½"

Twist.

❶

Using a threaded needle, join sleeves and body. Tie the threads loosely.

❷

Cut out collar using the pattern, and place it on the body. Overlap ends and glue at back.

Make head. Push toothpick into styrofoam ball. To make curly hair, make deep cuts into a short edge of the crepe paper, and wrap the ball with it. Press and smoth out the top, and glue to secure.

❹

Bring up "hair" and glue ends onto the crown, making the bang shorter. See below right for braided hair. Glue on bead eyes.

❺

Cut out the round hat and glue onto top of head to secure.

❻

Fold back edges and overlap at back; glue to secure.

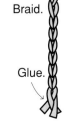

Braid.

Glue.

❼

Tie ribbon into a bow, and glue onto back of hat.

❽

Push toothpick into body to finish.

Braided hair

Wrap head with the wider strip of crepe paper. Make braids (see right) and glue onto head.

Approximate finished size: 3" W x 4" H

Materials per figure

Prepare **[K]**usudama pieces referring to pages 2-3.

2 3" square stiff wrapping paper for sleeves **[K]**

1 7" square stiff wrapping paper for body **[K]**

1 3" origami (white) for collar

1 1½" x 3½" crepe paper (brown) for hair

1 2" origami (blue) for hat

1 2" x 1½" thin colored card for music score

1 1" styrofoam ball for head

4" L #22 wrapped stem wire, cut into halves

2 2mm seed beads (black) for eyes, 1 (red) for mouth

1 wooden toothpick

Keys

△ = kusudama pc. ○ = styrofoam ball

- - - = Join with thread.

Numbers inside of △ indicate original size of the paper to be folded.

Assembly

← Hat

Head

← Collar

3" Sleeve

7" Body

Fold in half and insert edges into top of hat.

1/12" x 1/12"

Hat

Overlap about ¼" and glue.

Collar

LIFE SIZE PATTERN

Overlap about ½" and glue.

Trim with pinking shears.

❶ Using a threaded needle, join sleeves and body. Tie the threads loosely.

❷ Cut out collar using the pattern. Trim edges with pinking shears, and place it on the body. Overlap ends and glue at back.

❸ Make head. Push toothpick into styrofoam ball. Cut crepe paper into 1½"x 2½" strip, and glue onto ball. Pull together top edge and secure with glue.

Make bang. From remaining crepe paper, cut out ¾" x1¼". Round top end, and glue over the hair, smoothing the top.

❹

❺ Attach eyes and mouth. Make holes with toothpick, and bury beads with little glue.

❻ Make hat according to pattern, and glue onto head at a slant. Push toothpick into body.

❼ Attach arms. Bend 2" wire, insert one end into sleeve, and glue to secure. Repeat to make the other arm.

Make music by folding 2" x 1½" origami in half, and make center crease. Insert arms between the folds, and glue to secure.

❽

3 Choristers

Cute singing girls with petit berets set at a slant.
Seed beads can give features and wrapped stem
wire can be shaped into any angle.

Instructions: page 9

4 Dancing in the Rain

Quick to make cheerful dolls need only 4 kusudama pieces each. Balancing a mobile is fun, and the slightest breeze or draught will let each figure dance in the air.

Instructions: page 12

4. Dancing in the Rain on page 11

Approximate finished size: 16" W x 18" H

Materials

Prepare [K]usudama pieces referring to pages 2-3.

16 3" square wrapping paper for sleeves/hats/umbrella [K]

 8 4" square wrapping paper for bodies/umbrellas [K]

 5 2" origami (silver) for collars

 5 2" origami (blue) for boots

 5 ½" styrofoam balls for heads

 5 10" L #28 wrapped stem wire

 4 3" L fine pipe cleaners for umbrella handles

 4 12" L thin wooden rod

Assembly

LIFE SIZE PATTERN

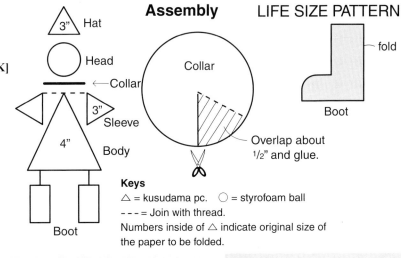

△ 3" Hat

○ Head

Collar

← Collar

3" Sleeve

4" Body

Boot

fold

Boot

Overlap about ½" and glue.

Keys

△ = kusudama pc.   ○ = styrofoam ball

- - - = Join with thread.

Numbers inside of △ indicate original size of the paper to be folded.

Mobile Structure

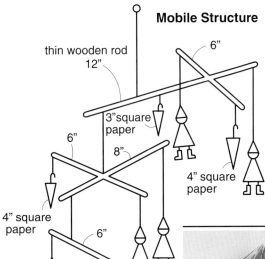

thin wooden rod 12"

6"

3"square paper

6"

8"

4" square paper

4" square paper

6"

4" square paper

Begin hanging with the lowest row, and carefully check the balance as you work upwards.

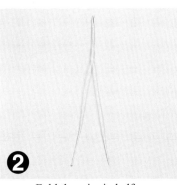

❶ Glue 2 small kusudama pieces onto sides of a large kusudama piece. Align the pleats.

❷ Fold the wire in half.

❸ Trim off tip of body, and insert ends of wire allowing some for head and hat.

❹ Make collar using the pattern. Place it on the body, and join ends with glue.

❺ Pierce the wire into styrofoam ball.

❻ Trim off tip of a small kusudama part for hat, and pierce with the wire.

❼ Secure a wire leg by gluing it in the fold of a body pleat. Glue the other wire leg onto the inner pleat on the opposite side.

❽ Fold paper for boot in half. Cut out the shape using the pattern. Insert wire legs into it and glue to secure. Repeat with the other boot. Make 5 dolls.

❾ Make 4 umbrellas. Insert and glue tip of pipe cleaner into 1 small kusudama piece. Repeat with 3 large kusudama pieces. Attach figures to rods cut into sizes using cotton thread. Each piece of thread should be a different length to add variety to the positions.

5. Balancing Clown on page 14

Assembly

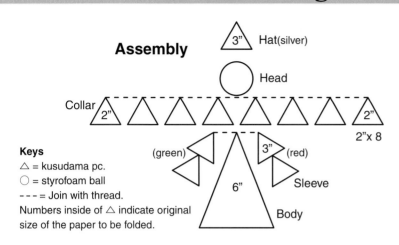

Hat(silver) 3"

Head

Collar 2" ... 2"
2"x 8

(green) 3" (red)

Sleeve

6"

Body

Keys
△ = kusudama pc.
◯ = styrofoam ball
- - - = Join with thread.
Numbers inside of △ indicate original
size of the paper to be folded.

Approximate finished size: 7" W x 10" H
Materials per figure
Prepare [K]usudama pieces referring to pages 2-3.
8 2" origami for collar [K]
2 3" origami (each red and green) for sleeves [K]
1 3" origami (silver) for hat [K]
1 6" square wrapping paper for body [K]
1 2½" x 3½" crepe paper for hair
9 ⅜" pompons (red)
1 1¼" styrofoam ball for head
2'4" L ¹/₁₂" aluminum craft wire
1 2mm seed bead for eye
1 3mm seed bead for mouth
2 star-shaped sequins
2 marbles for weights
1 wooden toothpick

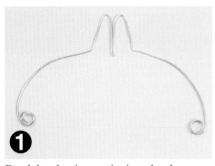

❶ Bend the aluminum wire into the shape
as shown. Curl ends around your finger.

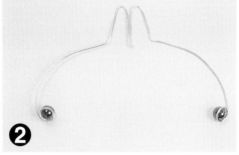

❷ Put marbles into the loops.

❸ Make ruffled sleeves by inserting a red
kusudama piece into the other red kusudama
piece. Glue to secure. Make the other ruffled
sleeve with green pieces. Join them with body
with threaded needle, and tie threads loosely.

❹ Make head. Push toothpick into styrofoam ball. Cut ⅛" wide
slits into a long side of crepe paper. Wrap it around the ball,
and round off the top, pulling creases together.

❺ Bring up "hair" and glue
ends onto the top of head.

Place the hat and glue to secure.
Make features by gluing beads
and sequins. Make a hole for the
eye before burying the bead.

❻

❼ Make collar. Join 8 kusudama
pieces to form a circle (see Steps ❷
and ❸ on page 4). Put the circle on
body, and then insert the head into
the center of it.

Glue on pompons as appropriate.

❽

❾ Insert the "W" section of the wire into the body
so that each "V" stays in the pleat on the
opposite side. Check the balance.

13

5 Balancing Clowns

A charming balancing toy making the most of
lightweight paper and styrofoam ball.
Shiny marbles make lovely weights.

Instructions: page 13

6 Clowns in Tears

Layers of metallic paper and solid origami paper create a colorful outfit for the sad clown.

Instructions: page 16

6. Clowns in Tears on page 15

Approximate finished size: 10" W x 8 " H
Materials per figure
Prepare [K]usudama pieces referring to pages 2-3.
8 2" origami in bright color for collar [K]
3 3" origami in bright color for sleeves [K]
3 4" origami in bright color for legs [K]
1 6" origami in bright color for body [K]
4 3" square wrapping paper for sleeves/hat [K]
3 4" square wrapping paper for legs [K]
1 6" square wrapping paper for body [K]
2 1/2" x 3 1/2" crepe paper for hair
5 5/8" pompons in matching color
1 1" styrofoam ball for head
1 2mm seed bead for eye
1 3mm seed bead for mouth
1 star-shaped sequin
1 wooden toothpick

Keys

△ = kusudama pc.　○ = styrofoam ball

- - - = Join with thread.

Numbers inside of △ indicate original size of the paper to be folded.

Assembly

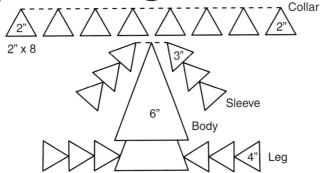

3" Hat

Head

Collar

2" x 8

3" Sleeve

6" Body

4" Leg

❶

Make sleeves and legs. Layer patterned kusudama piece and solid piece alternately, 3 layers each. Align pleats and glue to secure so the bottom pieces peek out about 5/8".

❷

Using a threaded needle, join sleeves and body. Knot ends loosely.

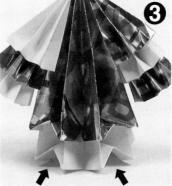

❸

For sitting clown, fold up the valley fold next to the front pleats into a small triangle. Fold the outer gown in the same manner. Repeat on the other side.

❹

Insert legs and glue to secure. See bottom right for legs of standing clown.

❹'

For standing clown, just insert and glue each leg into the pleats of body.

❺

Make collar. Join 8 kusudama pieces with a threaded needle, and knot tightly. Apply a dab of glue to top of the body, and put the collar on it.

❻

Make head. Push toothpick into styrofoam ball. Cut 1/8" wide slits into a long side of crepe paper. Wrap it around the ball, and glue the top onto head, pulling creases together.

❼

Make features by gluing on sequin and beads. Glue on hat, and top with pompon.

❽

Insert the toothpick into body, and glue to secure. Attach pompons to the ends of arms and legs for completed clown.

16

8. Chubby Pierrot on page 19

Approximate finished size: 6" W x 10" H

Materials

Prepare [K]usudama pieces referring to pages 2-3.

40 5" origami in gradated colors for ball [reverse K]
14 3" origami in gradated colors for sleeves [K] (2 sets of 7 colors)
10 3" origami for collar [K]
 1 6" origami (silver glitter) for hat [K]
 1 2$\frac{1}{2}$" x 8" crepe paper for hair
 3 2$\frac{1}{2}$" x 4" crepe paper for hair
 1 2" origami (red) for mouth
 1 2" origami (black) for eyes
 2 6" square origami (brown) for shoes
6" square corrugated board for shoes
 1 $\frac{3}{8}$" pompon (red) for nose
 2 $\frac{5}{8}$" pompons (pink) for hands
 1 $\frac{5}{8}$" pompon (blue) for hat
 1 2$\frac{1}{2}$" styrofoam ball for head
 2 $\frac{1}{2}$" joggle eyes
 2 star-shaped sequins for face
 1 bamboo skewer or thin wooden rod

Keys

△ = kusudama pc.
○ = styrofoam ball
- - - = Join with thread.
Numbers inside of △ indicate original size of the paper to be folded.

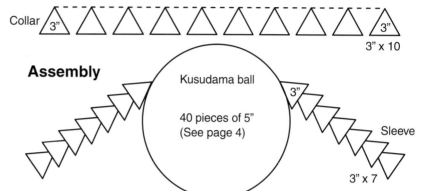

Hat /6"
Head ○

Collar /3" △ △ △ △ △ △ △ △ /3"
3" x 10

Assembly

Kusudama ball

40 pieces of 5"
(See page 4)

3"

3"

Sleeve

3" x 7

LIFE SIZE PATTERN

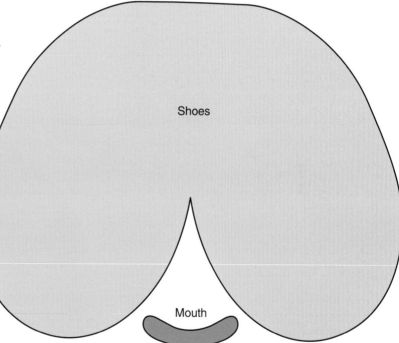

Shoes

Mouth

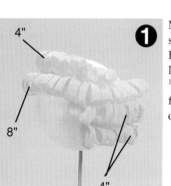

4"

8"

4"

❶ Make head. Push bamboo skewer into styrofoam ball. Fold crepe paper strips lengthwise in half, and cut $\frac{1}{4}$" deep slits all along the fold. Glue the other ends onto head.

❷ Make hat. Make a kusudama piece. Make its bottom as flat as possible by pinching a mountain fold next to a thicker fold, and pressing its white side to crease. Repeat with remaining 3 thin folds.

❸

Place the hat on head. Glue joggle eyes onto black origami, and trim all around. Glue them onto face. Attach sequins. Cut out mouth shape using pattern, and glue. Attach pompon onto nose position.

Join 10 kusudama pieces for collar with threaded needle, to form a circle. Checking the balance of the kusudama ball, place the circle on top of it. Stack 7 sleeve pieces of different colors. Make 2. Insert sleeves into sides.

❹

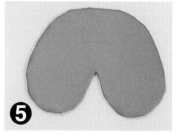

❺

From corrugated board, cut out shoes shape. Wrap it with brown origami to cover, and glue edges. Insert the bamboo skewer through the body into the shoes so the whole figure stands on its own. Glue to secure.

7 Performing Pierrots

Sitting pierrot has free-moving legs while standing one can be balanced with inner wire.

Instructions: page 20

8 Chubby Pierrot

Jovial clown balanced on big shoes.

Instructions: page 17

7. Performing Pierrots on page 18

Approximate finished size: 4" W x 6"- 7"H
Materials per figure
Prepare [K]usudama pieces referring to pages 2-3.
40 5" double-sided origami for kusudama ball [K]
  8 2" origami (solid color) for collar[K]
  3 3" square wrapping paper for hat/sleeves[K]
  2 4" square wrapping paper for legs[K]
  1 6" square wrapping paper for body[K]
1¼" x 3" crepe paper for hair
  3 ½" pompons for hat/body
  2 ⅝" pompons for hands
  2 ⅝" pompons for feet
  1 1" styrofoam ball for head
5" L and 7" L #22 wrapped wire for standing pierrot
  2 3mm seed beads for eyes and mouth
  1 star-shaped sequin for face
  2 wooden toothpicks

Assembly

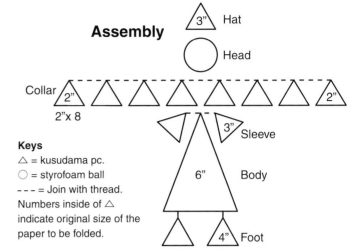

Keys
△ = kusudama pc.
○ = styrofoam ball
- - - = Join with thread.
Numbers inside of △
indicate original size of the
paper to be folded.

Make kusudama ball referring
to page 4, using 40 kusudama
pieces.

Sitting Pierrot

❶

Make legs. From inside of a 4"
kusudama piece, pierce top with
threaded needle. Tie a large knot.

❷

Make body, and pierce one of
its bottom pleats with the thread
extended from leg.

❸

Knot, leaving some extra length,
and apply glue to the knot.
Repeat with the other leg.

❹

Using threaded needle, join
sleeves and body. Tie the
threads loosely.

❺

Make collar. Using threaded
needle, join all 8 kusudama
pieces in the round.

❻

Apply a dab of glue to top
of body, and attach collar.

❼

Make head. Push toothpick into
styrofoam ball. Wrap the ball
with crepe paper at a slant, and
glue to secure.

❽

Apply glue to the bottom of
hat, and attach to the head.
Glue a smaller pompon on
top of head.

❾

Using a toothpick or any pointed
tool, make holes to bury beads
for eye and mouth. Glue on a
star-shaped sequin as an eye.

Apply a dab of glue to center of collar,
and insert the toothpick into it.

❿

⓫

Glue pompons onto body and
ends of sleeves and legs to finish.

9. Mademoiselle on page 22

Assembly

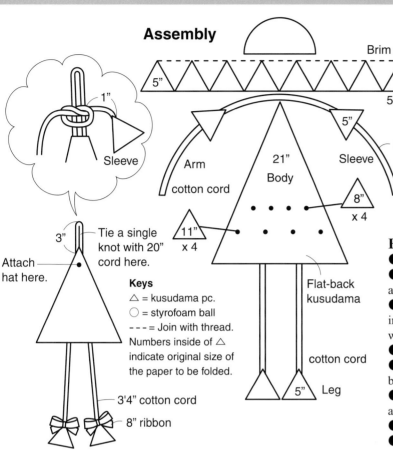

Brim

5"

5"

5" x 8

5"

20"

Arm

cotton cord

21"
Body

Sleeve

Sleeve

8"
x 4

11"
x 4

3"

Attach
hat here.

Tie a single
knot with 20"
cord here.

Flat-back
kusudama

cotton cord

1"

Sleeve

Keys
△ = kusudama pc.
○ = styrofoam ball
- - - = Join with thread.
Numbers inside of △
indicate original size of
the paper to be folded.

3'4" cotton cord

8" ribbon

5" Leg

Approximate finished size: 13" W x 40" H
Materials
Prepare [K]usudama pieces referring to pages 2-3.
Prepare [K*]usudama pieces referring to page 22.
  1 21" square wrapping paper (tartan) for body [K*]
  4 11" square wrapping paper for front ruffles [K]
  4 8" square wrapping paper for front ruffles [K]
 12 5 " square wrapping paper for hat [K]
  1 7" square wrapping paper for hat
  1 3¼" styrofoam ball, cut in half
  5' ³⁄₈" cotton cord (white) for limbs
 38" L ⁵⁄₈"W ribbon, cut into 2 8" and 1 22" lengths
 Miniature silk flower bouquet
 1 bamboo skewer or thin wooden rod

Brief Instructions
● Make body referring to instructions on page 22.
● Make sleeves and feet. Trim ¹⁄₂" off the tops of body, sleeves and feet.
● Cut 3'4" length of cotton cord, and fold in half. Insert its fold into body so 3" loop extends from the top. Tie the loop one time with remaining cord.
● Insert ends of the cord into sleeves and legs, and glue to secure.
● Make hat. Join 8 pieces to form a circle. Wrap halved styrofoam ball with extra wrapping paper, and glue onto the hat circle.
● Tie ribbon around the hat, into a bow. Tie short ribbon strips to ankles.
● Glue the completed hat to body. Glue front ruffles in tiers.
● Tie a knot with arms, and glue on bouquet.

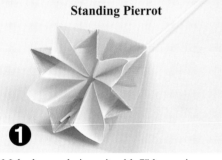

Standing Pierrot

❶

Make leg, and pierce it with 7" long wire. Glue wire to inside of pleat, allowing 5" length above the leg.

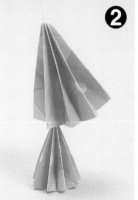

❷ Attach the leg to body, by gluing the extending length of wire onto inside of pleat.

Make the other leg in the same manner using 5" long wire, and attach larger pompons to its bottom.

❸

❹ Using threaded needle, join sleeves and body. Tie the threads loosely. (See Steps ❺ - ⓬ for details)

❺ Make collar. Join 8 collar pieces to form a circle. Apply a dab of glue to top of the body and attach this collar.

Trim any excess wire. Apply a dab of glue to center of collar, and insert the toothpick into it. Glue on pompons to finish.

❻

21

9 Mademoiselle

Cute wall-hanging doll with flat back and 3-D frilled front.

Instructions: page 21

Flat-back kusudama [K*] for body

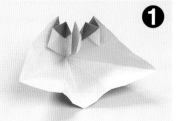

❶ Work Steps ❶ to ⓲ on pages 2 and 3 for kusudama folding.

❷ Continue folding on next section but only on one side. Repeat on the other section.

❸ Using the creases, fold in the triangle.

❹ Repeat on the other side.

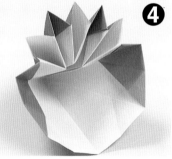

❺ Hold the middle pleat, and bring to one side.

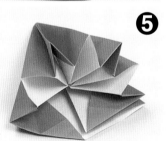

❻ Staple side pleats flat to let the 3 mountain folds stand out.

10 Easter Bunny

Unexpectedly easy. Pieces are only glued together with glue gun.

Side View

Assembly

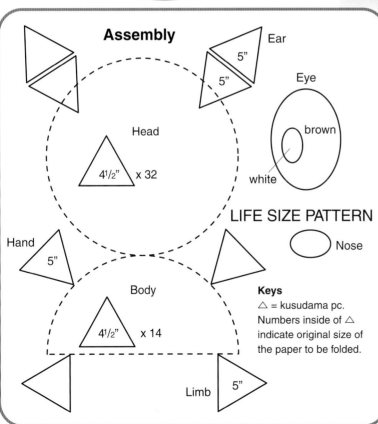

Ear

△ 5"

△ 5"

Eye

brown

white

Head

△ 4¹/₂" x 32

LIFE SIZE PATTERN

○ Nose

Hand

△ 5"

Body

△ 4¹/₂" x 14

Keys
△ = kusudama pc.
Numbers inside of △
indicate original size of
the paper to be folded.

Limb △ 5"

Approximate finished size: 7" W x 1' H
Materials
Prepare [K]usudama pieces referring to pages 2 - 3.
46 4¹/₂" square wrapping paper (solid) for head/body **[K]**
 8 5" square wrapping paper (pattern) for ears/limbs **[K]**
1¹/₄" x 2¹/₂" felt (brown) for eyes/nose
¹/₂" x ³/₄" felt (white) for eyes
6 2" L pipe cleaners for whiskers

Brief Instructions
● Make head. Using glue gun, form a ball of 32 kusudama pieces, each made of 4¹/₂" square sheet of paper.(page 4)
● Make body. Form a circle with 8 pieces, each made of 4¹/₂" square sheet of paper, and form a dome shape by gluing remaining pieces.
● Place head on body, and glue together checking the balance as you work.
● Glue ears symmetrically onto head.
● Cut out eye and nose shapes from felt, and attach them with glue. Attach whiskers by inserting pipe cleaners, 3 on each side.

HOW TO FOLD A BELLFLOWER PIECE

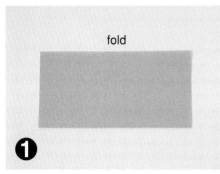

1 Fold in half, white side facing in.

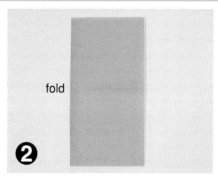

2 Unfold and fold in half again.

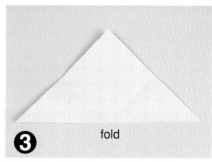

3 Unfold and fold diagonally in half, colored side facing in.

4 Unfold and fold diagonally crossways.

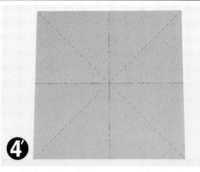

4' Unfold, colored side up, and check that there are short creases of mountain folds, and longer diagonal creases of valley folds.

5 Push up the center.

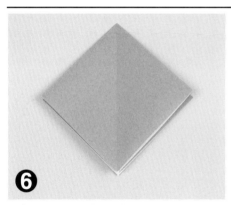

6 Using creases, collapse into a square.

7 Fold in an upper diagonal fold to align with the center.

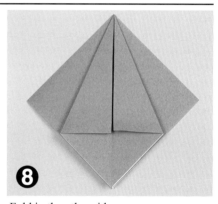

8 Fold in the other side.

9 Turn over and repeat.

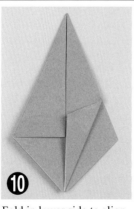

10 Fold in lower side to align with the center lines.

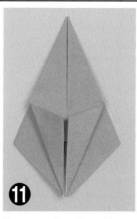

11 Repeat on the other side.

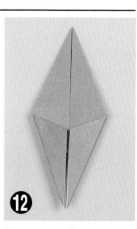

12 Turn over and repeat.

Bellflower pieces are used to form puffy sleeves or skirts.

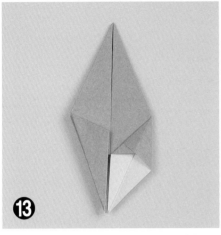

13 Unfold lower side, and squash carefully and precisely. Repeat on the other side.

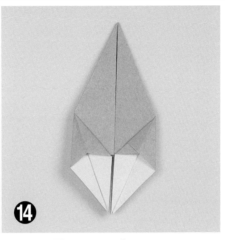

14 Turn over and repeat.

15 Fold one side across to work on smooth plane.

16 Fold in lower side to align with the center.

Repeat on the other side.

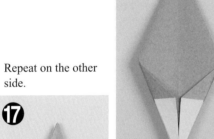

17

18 Turn over and repeat.

Fold up bottom triangle, aligning the center lines.

19

20 Fold one side across and repeat. Repeat on remaining sides.

Open out into a bellflower.

21

A-Finish

22 Secure the triangular flaps with glue.

B-Finish

22 Fold the triangular flaps inside, and secure with glue.

C-Finish

22 Curl the triangular flaps by wrapping each around a tooth pick or thin rod.

25

11 The Baron

The "bellflower" pieces made into a hat and gown with great pump.

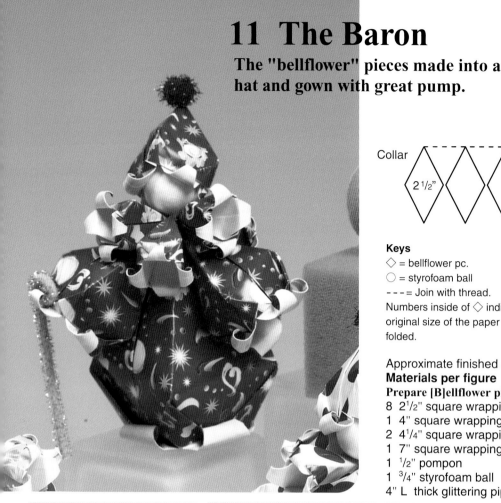

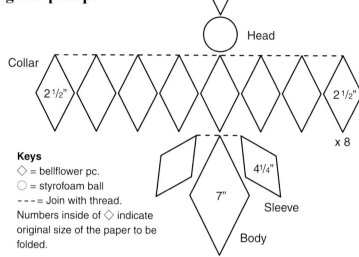

Hat 4"

Head

Collar

2 1/2"

2 1/2"

x 8

Sleeve 4 1/4"

Body 7"

Keys

◇ = bellflower pc.
◯ = styrofoam ball
‐‐‐‐ = Join with thread.
Numbers inside of ◇ indicate original size of the paper to be folded.

Approximate finished size: 4" W x 6" H

Materials per figure

Prepare [B]ellflower pieces referring to pages 24-25.

8 2 1/2" square wrapping paper for collar [B]
1 4" square wrapping paper for hat [B]
2 4 1/4" square wrapping paper for sleeves [B]
1 7" square wrapping paper for body [B]
1 1/2" pompon
1 3/4" styrofoam ball
4" L thick glittering pipe cleaner, 1 wooden toothpick

❶ Referring to pages 24 and 25, prepare bellflower pieces with C-Finish .

❷ Using a threaded needle, join sleeves through body. Pierce body through mountain fold to mountain fold on the opposite side. Tie the threads loosely.

❸ Make collar. Thread 8 collar bellflower pieces made of 2 1/2" squares.

❹ Pull thread and knot tightly to form a circle.

❺ Place collar on body.

❻ Glue pompon onto tip of hat piece. Push toothpick into styrofoam ball. Holding the toothpick in one hand, put the hat at a slant.

❼ Apply glue onto center of collar, and insert end of toothpick. Form a walking stick with pipe cleaner, and hook onto end of sleeve to finish.

WORLD OF FAIRIES
12 Gnomes

Bellflower folding is used to form the bodies of these cute and plump gnomes. Enjoy eyecatching combinations of double-face origami paper.

Instructions: page 28

12. Gnomes on page 27

Approximate finished size: 2¹/₂" W x 5" H
Materials per figure
Prepare [K]usudama pieces referring to pages 2-3.
Prepare [B]ellflower pieces referring to pages 24-25.
2 2" origami for body/hat (match with body) **[K]**
2 2¹/₂" double-sided origami for sleeves **[K]**
1 5" double-sided origami for body **[B]**
1 2" origami for collar
³/₄" x 3" crepe paper (brown) for hair
3" x 4" construction paper (brown) for boots
1 ³/₄" styrofoam ball for head
2 10" L #22 wrapped wire
2 2mm seed beads for eyes, 1 3mm seed bead for mouth

Assembly

Hat 2"
Head
Collar
2¹/₂"
Sleeve
2"
Body
5"
wire
Boot

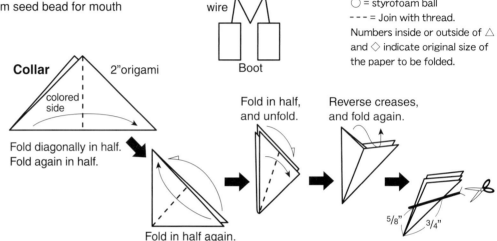

LIFE SIZE PATTERN

Keys
△ = kusudama pc.
◇ = bellflower pc.
○ = styrofoam ball
- - - = Join with thread.
Numbers inside or outside of △
and ◇ indicate original size of
the paper to be folded.

Collar 2"origami
colored side
Fold diagonally in half.
Fold again in half.
Fold in half again.
Fold in half, and unfold.
Reverse creases, and fold again.
5/8" 3/4"

❶
Make body. Fold a bellflower
piece with A-Finish, referring to
pages 24 and 25.

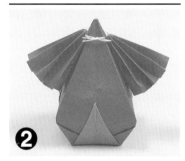

❷
Using a threaded needle, join
sleeves of kusudama pieces and
body. Tie the threads loosely.

❸
Make collar. Fold diagonally
in half 3 times to make 16
radial creases. (right)

❹
Make head. Attach eyes and mouth to
styrofoam ball and push a toothpick
into it. Wrap around with crepe paper,
press down top, and glue to secure.

❺
Glue on hat made from 2"
square paper.

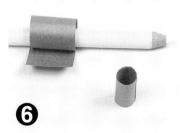

❻
Make boots. Curl construction
paper cut into ³/₄" x 3" around a
pencil or rod by wrapping tightly
around it. Secure end with glue.

❼
Cut out upper using life-size
pattern. Wrap it around the
cylinder made in Step **❻**.

❽
Laminate 2 sheets of ³/₄" squares,
and lay flat. Place boot on it, and
glue to secure.

❾
Trim edges to finish boot.
Make 2.

28

Keys

△ = kusudama pc.
◯ = styrofoam ball
Numbers inside of △ indicate original size of the paper to be folded.

Santa's Face

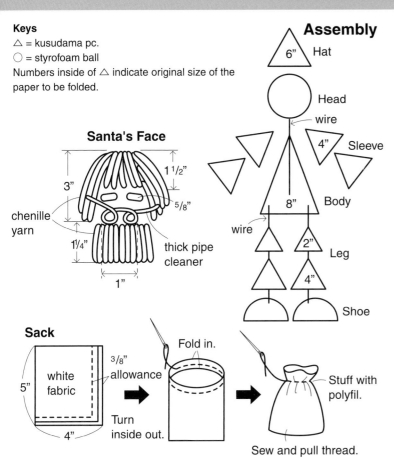

- 3"
- 1 1/2"
- 5/8"
- 1 1/4"
- 1"

chenille yarn

thick pipe cleaner

Assembly

6" Hat
Head
wire
4" Sleeve
8" Body
wire
2" Leg
4"
Shoe

Sack

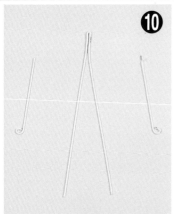

white fabric
5"
4"
3/8" allowance
Turn inside out.
Fold in.
Stuff with polyfil.
Sew and pull thread.

Approximate finished size: 6" W x 11" H

Materials

Prepare [K]usudama pieces referring to pages 2-3.
- 1 8" square each red fabric and card for body [K]
- 1 6" square each fabric and card for hat [K]
- 6 4" square each fabric and card for sleeves/legs [K]
- 2 2" square each red fabric and card for legs [K]
- 2 3 1/4" square red fabric for shoes [K]
- 2 2" styrofoam balls, 1 cut into halves
- Chenille yarn and thick pipe cleaners (white)
- 5" L 1/16" craft wire for eyeglasses (gold)
- #18 wrapped wire, cut into 1 3" and 2 4 1/2" lengths
- 8" x 5" white fabric, Polyfil

Brief Instructions

● Laminate fabric and paper with glue before folding kusudama pieces.
● Make shoes. Halve styrofoam ball, and wrap each with red fabric.
● Cut 2 pieces of 4 1/2" wire and push each into shoes.
● Make head by attaching chenille yarn and pipe cleaner as illustrated. Push 3" long wrapped wire into head, and through to body.
● Push upper ends of wire into body. Stack sleeve pieces and glue, using glue gun.
● Place hat on head. Trim hat and jacket hem with pipe cleaner.
● Make 3 buttons by curling ends of pipe cleaners into 5/8" circle. Attach them to hat and center front. Make sack and put on shoulder.

---

❿ Prepare wire. Cut two 2" lengths of wrapped wire for arms. Curl one end of each wire. Make legs by folding 10" length of wire in half.

Make a hole in pointed end of body, and insert folded end of wire. To reinforce top of body, insert a kusudama piece (2" origami) and glue together.

⓫

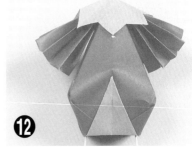

⓬

Attach collar: Make a slit and wrap around top of body. Overlap edges and glue.

⓭ Attach head. Remove toothpick. Apply glue onto end of wire, and insert into head.

Bend wire arms and glue each onto inner pleats of sleeve.

⓮

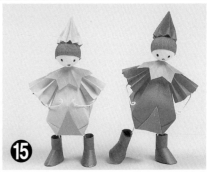

⓯

Insert wire ends into boots, and adjust to balance.

WORLD OF FAIRIES

13 Fat Santa

A warm atmosphere is created with fuzzy features made of white pipe cleaner and chenille yarn.

Instructions: page 29

14 Christmas Tree

Texture of thick crepe paper gives a feeling of calm and weight to this tree. Decorate freely.

Instructions: page 32

15 White Christmas

**An elegantly tall Christmas tree made
of crisp tracing paper or parchment.**

Instructions: page 33

16 Dressed-up Santa

**Note the combination of large/small
and red/white kusudama pieces.**

Instructions: page 32

31

14. Christmas Tree on page 30

Approximate finished size: 10" W x 16" H

Materials

Prepare [K]usudama pieces referring to pages 2-3.

1 21" square thick crepe paper **[K]**
8 8" square thick crepe paper **[K]**
5 6" square thick crepe paper **[K]**
19 ½" pompons (glittering white)
4 10" L fine pipe cleaners (each gold and silver)
10 5" L fine pipe cleaners (silver)
#30 wire (gold), cut into 2" lengths
2' 8"L ½" ribbon, cut into 6
Sequins, 1 bow ornament
12" x 12" corrugated board, cut into 12" x 3", 6" x 12", 3" x 12"

Brief Instructions

● Tightly roll 12" long board into a tube of 1" diameter. Roll remaining boards as illustrated to make base. Color the base in brown.
● Set largest kusudama piece over the base, and glue to secure. Beginning from bottom, glue large kusudama pieces all around the tree, then small kusudama pieces onto valley folds of the tree.
● Shape 10" pipe cleaners into a wave form. Attach them to the tree alternating gold and silver. Form a star shape with 5" pipe cleaner and attach to top. Attach ornament onto it.
● Make 9 tiny bows using silver pipe cleaners and ribbon as shown, and attach to the tree.
● Glue on pompons and sequins in a balanced manner.

Base corrugated board

12"
6"
1" in diam. 2½"in diam.
2½"
3"
3"
Color in brown.

Keys
△ = kusudama pc.
Numbers inside of △ indicate original size of the paper to be folded.

Assembly

6"
6" x 4
21"
8" x 8

Bow
1"
5" fine pipe cleaners (silver)
2" wire
1" ribbon

16. Dressed-up Santa on page 31

Approximate finished size: 6" W x 12" H

Materials

Prepare [K]usudama pieces referring to pages 2-3.

1 6" origami (red) for body **[K]**
1 5" origami (red) for hat **[K]**
6 4" origami (white) for peplum **[K]**
10 3½" origami (red) for legs/sleeves **[K]**
2 3½" origami (white) for legs **[K]**
10 3" origami (each red and white) for collar/sleeves **[K]**
8 2" origami (white) for hair **[K]**
1 1½" styrofoam ball for head
1 1" styrofoam ball for feet
12" x 6" felt (white)
1½"L 1" fake fur tape
1 ½" pompon (white)
2 10" L #16 wrapped wire
Board

Brief Instructions

● Make shoes. Halve the styrofoam ball, color in black, and push wire into each. Stack kusudama pieces for leg by inserting the wire. Make 2 and adjust lengths.
● Using threaded needle, join peplum pieces. Place legs in position, and set peplum by inserting wires.
● Add body. Add 2 layers of collar made of 8 pieces each, joined with thread.
● Set styrofoam head. Join 8 pieces for hair in the round, and glue onto head. Glue on hat. Glue pompon onto its tip.
● Glue on sleeves by stacking 3 pieces on each side.
● Make felt sack, and sew onto edge of a sleeve.
● Glue on fur tape to make beard.

Keys
△ = kusudama pc.
○ = styrofoam ball
- - - = Join with thread.
Numbers inside or outside of △ indicate original size of the paper to be folded.

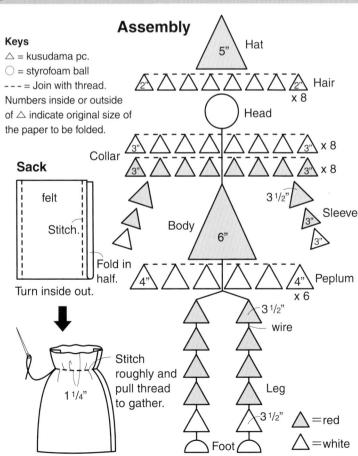

Assembly
5" Hat
2" Hair 2" x 8
Head
Collar 3" 3" x 8
3" 3" x 8
3½"
Body 6" Sleeve 3" 3"
4" 4" Peplum x 6
3½" wire
3½"
Leg
3½"
Foot

△ = red
△ = white

Sack
felt
Stitch.
Fold in half.
Turn inside out.

Stitch roughly and pull thread to gather.
1¼"

17. Anne of Green Gables   on page 34

Keys
△ = kusudama pc.
◇ = bellflower pc.
◯ = styrofoam ball
- - - = Join with thread.
Numbers inside or outside of △ and ◇ indicate original size of the paper to be folded.

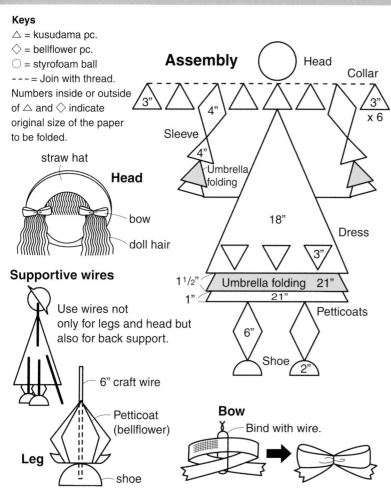

Assembly Head

straw hat

Head

bow

doll hair

Collar

3"

4"

Sleeve

4"

Umbrella folding

x 6

3"

18"

Dress

3"

Supportive wires

Use wires not only for legs and head but also for back support.

6" craft wire

Petticoat (bellflower)

Leg

shoe

1 1/2"

1"

Umbrella folding   21"

21"

Petticoats

6"

Shoe

2"

Bow Bind with wire.

Approximate finished size: 8" W x 16" H
Materials
Prepare [K]usudama pieces referring to pages 2-3.
Prepare [B]ellflower pieces referring to pages 24-25.
1 18" square wrapping paper for dress [K]
2 4" square wrapping paper for sleeves [K]
2 4" square wrapping paper for upper sleeves [B]
9 3" square wrapping paper for collar [K]
9 3" square washi paper for collar [K]
2 4" square washi paper for sleeves
1 21" square washi paper for petticoat [K]
1 21" square wax paper (brown) for petticoat [K]
2 4" square wax paper (brown) for sleeves [K]
2 6" square wrapping paper for bloomers [B]
1 2 1/2" strofoam ball for head
1 2" styrofoam ball for shoes
3' 4" L $5/8$" ribbon (gingham)
2' L 1" cotton lace ribbon
8" square crepe paper for shoes
4 6" L $1/8$" craft wire
Doll hair, 6" straw hat, Mascot bunny, Pinking shears

Brief Instructions
● Prepare umbrella pieces with 4" and 21" square washi papers (page 60.) Trim edges into scallop hem using pinking shears. Layer small umbrellas with other sleeve pieces, large umbrella between dress and petticoat to peek between them. Glue to secure.
● Make collar. Layer washi and wrapping paper edge to edge, and fold into kusudama piece. Join 6 pieces with thread, adding bellflower sleeves referring to diagram.
● Place collar on top of dress. Make head as illustrated, and push a wire into it. Insert wire into dress, and tie a cotton ribbon around neck.
● Halve styrofoam ball, and wrap each with crepe paper to make shoes. Into each shoe, push craft wire. Pierce each wire into bloomer piece. Insert wires into dress to secure.
● Glue on layered sleeves. Glue on mascot bunny.

15. White Christmas   on page 31

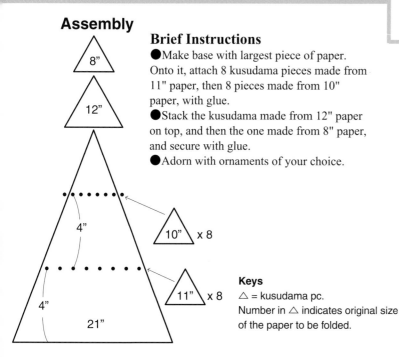

Assembly

8"

12"

4"

4"

10" x 8

11" x 8

4"

21"

Brief Instructions
● Make base with largest piece of paper. Onto it, attach 8 kusudama pieces made from 11" paper, then 8 pieces made from 10" paper, with glue.
● Stack the kusudama made from 12" paper on top, and then the one made from 8" paper, and secure with glue.
● Adorn with ornaments of your choice.

Keys
△ = kusudama pc.
Number in △ indicates original size of the paper to be folded.

Approximate finished size: 10" W x 15" H
Materials
Prepare [K]usudama pieces referring to pages 2-3.
1 21" square tracing paper [K]
1 12" square tracing paper [K]
8 11" square tracing paper [K]
8 10" square tracing paper [K]
1 8" square tracing paper [K]
#30 wire (gold), cut into 2" lengths
32" L $3/4$" ribbon, cut into 4
Christmas ornaments such as:
  star garland, snowmen, etc.

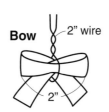

Bow 2" wire

2"

17 Anne of Green Gables

Select patterned paper to create the mood of an early American dress.

Instructions: page 33

Side View

18 Flower Nymphs

Tiered floral dress with bell sleeves, accented with cute frilled collar. Choose paper of soft shades.

Instructions: page 37

19. English Roses on page 38

Approximate finished size: 6" W x 8" H
Materials per figure
Prepare [K]usudama pieces referring to pages 2-3.
12 2" square wrapping paper (floral) **[K]**
10 3" square wrapping paper (floral) **[K]**
 1 12" square wrapping paper (floral) for body **[K]**
1 ³/₄" styrofoam ball for head
2 wooden toothpicks

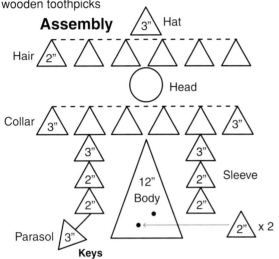

Assembly

Keys
△ = kusudama pc.   ○ = styrofoam ball
- - - = Join with thread.
Numbers inside of △ indicate original size
of the paper to be folded.

❶ With double-threaded needle, pierce a tip of small kusudama piece, at ¹/₁₆" to ¹/₈" from the pointed end.

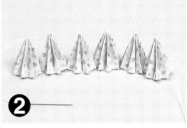

❷ Join 6 pieces of the same size kusudama by piercing each tip.

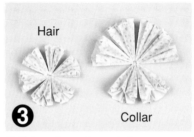

❸ Pull thread to make a circle. Repeat with 6 medium pieces of kusudama.

❹ Make sleeves. Insert a small kusudama piece into a medium piece, aligning the pleats. Alternate single edge and folded edge so the thickness stays even all around.

❺ In the same manner, insert another small piece to finish sleeve. Secure with glue applied onto inner pleats. Make 2.

❻ Insert each sleeve into collar piece. Secure with glue applied onto inner pleats.

❼ Apply a dab of glue onto top of body.

❽ Place collar/sleeves made in Step ❻ onto it.

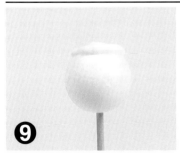

❾ Make head. Push a toothpick into styrofoam ball, and hold with one of your hand. Apply a dab of glue on top of head.

❿ Stick the circle of hair pieces at an angle. Hold them gently for a while until almost set.

⓫ Apply glue onto inside of hat piece, and put it over hair.

⓬ Apply glue onto pointed tip of toothpick, and insert into body.

36

18. Flower Nymphs on page 35

Approximate finished size: 4" W x 6" H
Materials per figure
Prepare [K]usudama pieces referring to pages 2-3.
Prepare [B]ellflower pieces referring to pages 24-25.
1 7" square wrapping paper (floral) for body **[K]**
1 8" square wrapping paper (floral) for body **[K]**
2 4" square wrapping paper (floral) for sleeves **[B]**
2 1¹/₂" x 10" tissue paper (pink) for collar
1 1¹/₂" x 2¹/₂" crepe paper (yellow) for hair
1 1¹/₄" x 1¹/₂" crepe paper (yellow) for hair
1 1" styrofoam ball for head
2 10" L #22 wrapped wire
2 2mm seed beads for eyes
Miniature flowers
2 wooden toothpicks

Assembly

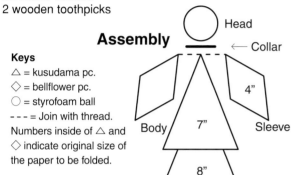

Keys
△ = kusudama pc.
◇ = bellflower pc.
○ = styrofoam ball
- - - = Join with thread.
Numbers inside of △ and
◇ indicate original size of
the paper to be folded.

Head
← Collar
4"
Body   7"   Sleeve
8"

① Make body. Insert smaller kusudama piece into large one. Adjust the layering so ¹/₂" pleats peak out, and glue to secure.

With threaded needle, pierce "bellflower" sleeve, body, then another "bellflower" sleeve. Tie loosely.

②

③ Make collar. Layer tissue paper, and fold narrow pleats. Push toothpick into center.

Unfold, and dot glue along center. Fold again to secure.

④

⑤ Unfold to form a disc. Glue end pleats together. Apply glue onto top of body, and push the toothpick of collar into it.

⑥ Push toothpick into styrofoam ball. Make hair. Using your fingernail, spread shrinks of crepe paper along edges to form flare. Glue onto head.

⑦ Press upper edges of crepe paper, and secure with glue. Make flared bang in the same manner as Step **⑥**, and glue on.

⑧ Make holes at eye positions using toothpick, and bury beads with little glue. Attach florets onto head.

⑬ Make parasol. Apply glue onto inside of kusudama piece, and insert a toothpick.

⑭ Apply glue onto inside of sleeve piece, and insert toothpick of parasol.

Adorn skirt with small 2 kusudama pieces glued between pleats.

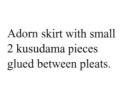

⑮

⑨ Remove toothpick from head, and insert the other toothpick extending from the body into it to finish.

GARDEN PARTY

19 English Roses

Pretty floral dresses are enhanced with smaller kusudama pieces including cute parasols.

Instructions: page 36

20 Edwardian Ladies
Double layers of ruff add up a classical touch.

Instructions: page 40

20. Edwardian Ladies on page 39

Approximate finished size: 4" W x 8" H
Materials per figure
Prepare [K]usudama pieces referring to pages 2-3.
18 2" square wrapping paper for hair/collar/sleeves [K]
 8 3" square wrapping paper for under-collar [K]
 1 12" square wrapping paper for body [K]
 1 3" square wrapping paper for purse
1 ³/₄" styrofoam ball for head
16" L ¹/₄" ribbon, cut into 11" and 5"
1 wooden toothpick

Hair

❶ Upper Collar

❷

❸

Using threaded needle, join 6 kusudama pieces for hair in the round. In the same manner, join 8 kusudama pieces for upper collar. Then make lower collar using 8 sheets of 3 " square paper.

Make sleeves by stacking 2 kusudama pieces, and insert them into lower collar, allowing 3 pieces between each. Secure with glue.

Apply a dab of glue to top of body, and put lower collar with sleeves.

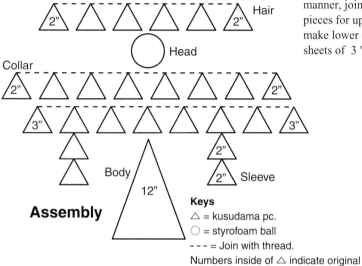

Hair
2" △ △ △ △ 2"

Head ◯

Collar
2" △ △ △ △ △ △ △ △ 2"
3" △ △ △ △ △ △ △ △ 3"
△ 2"
△ Body △ 2" Sleeve
△ 12"

Assembly

Keys
△ = kusudama pc.
◯ = styrofoam ball
- - - = Join with thread.
Numbers inside of △ indicate original size of the paper to be folded.

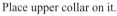

❹ Place upper collar on it.

❺ Push a toothpick into styrofoam ball, and insert its pointed end into center of collars and body.

❻ Glue on hair made in Step ❶ .

❼ Make a bow with ribbon, and glue onto top of hair.

❽ Make purse referring to illustrations below, and glue onto a sleeve to finish.

Purse

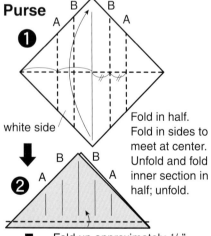

❶
B B
A A
white side

Fold in half. Fold in sides to meet at center. Unfold and fold inner section in half; unfold.

❷
B B
A A
Fold up approximately ¹/₄".

❸
B B
A A
Align with line B.

❹ Unfold.

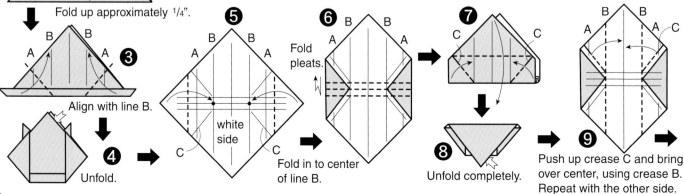

❺
B B
A A
white side
C C
Fold in to center of line B.

❻
B B
A A
Fold pleats.

❼
C C
❽ Unfold completely.

❾
B B
A A C
Push up crease C and bring over center, using crease B. Repeat with the other side.

21. Southern Belles on page 42

1 Make hair. Using threaded needle, join 3 smallest kusudama pieces and 4 pieces for hair, and pull thread to make a circle.

Approximate finished size: 3" W x 9" H
Materials per figure
Prepare [K]usudama pieces referring to pages 2-3.
Prepare [B]ellflower pieces referring to pages 24-25.
10 2" square wrapping paper for hair/collar **[K]**
 4 3" square wrapping paper for hair **[K]**
 2 3$\frac{1}{2}$" square wrapping paper for sleeves **[B]**
 1 5" square wrapping paper for bodice **[B]**
 1 10" square wrapping paper for skirt **[B]**
 1 9" square wrapping paper for underskirt **[K]**
 1 $\frac{3}{4}$" styrofoam ball for head
2'4" L $\frac{1}{2}$" sheer ribbon for hat
8" L $\frac{1}{4}$" ribbon for bouquet
2 3" L pipe cleaners for arms
Miniature bouquet, 1 wooden toothpick

Keys
△ = kusudama pc.   ◇ = bellflower pc.
○ = styrofoam ball   - - - = Join with thread.
Numbers inside of △ and ◇ indicate original size of the paper to be folded.

Hair

Head

Assembly

Standing collar

Collar

Sleeve (C-Finish)

Bodice (B-Finish)

Skirt (B-Finish)

Underskirt

2 Push toothpick into styrofoam ball. Apply a dab of glue onto top of styrofoam head, and gently wrap with hair pieces using all your fingers.

3 Join 3 kusudama pieces for collar with bellflower (C-Finish) sleeve, then repeat. Pull thread and tie a knot.

4 Apply a dab of glue onto top of bellflower (B-Finish) bodice, and place collar and sleeve sequence on it.

5 Make standing collar by trimming away pointed end of kusudama piece made from 2" square. Secure pleats with glue applied inside cut edges so the pleats will stay sharp.

6 Turn standing collar upside down. Apply a dab of glue onto center of collar, and insert head into it.

7 Apply glue generously onto bottom flaps of bellflower bodice.

8 Insert largest bellflower piece (B-Finish) for skirt into bodice. Then insert kusudama piece for underskirt into skirt. Redress the balance.

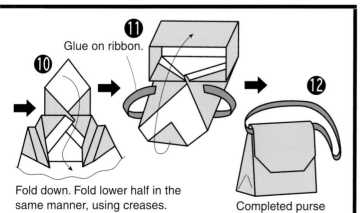

Glue on ribbon.

10

11

12

Fold down. Fold lower half in the same manner, using creases.

Completed purse

9 Make arms with pipe cleaners. Glue one end to inside of sleeve.

10 Hook the other ends of pipe cleaners to join each other. Put bouquet on the joint. Tie a ribbon bow, and attach to back of head.

21 Southern Belles

The fullness of skirt and sleeves are created with bellflower pieces.

Instructions: page 41

Mat surfaced tiered dress is a simple combination of kusudama and bellflower pieces.

Instructions: page 44

22. Velvet Damsels on page 43

Approximate finished size: 5" W x 10" H
Materials per figure
Prepare [K]usudama pieces referring to pages 2-3.
Prepare [B]ellflower pieces referring to pages 24-25.
1 3" square wrapping paper for hat [K]
2 4" square wrapping paper for sleeves [K]
1 6" square wrapping paper for bodice [K]
1 8" square wrapping paper for skirt [K]
1 10" square wrapping paper for skirt [K]
8 2" origami (same tone as body) for collar [K]
2 4" square wrapping paper for sleeves [B]
2 4" square wrapping paper for hat
1¼" x 3½" crepe paper (brown) for hair
1 2" styrofoam ball for head
24" L ¼" ribbon (gold)
Miniature flowers, 1 wooden toothpick

❶ Insert a kusudama piece for sleeve into a bellflower (B-Finish) piece. Glue inside to secure.

❷ Make body by stacking 3 body pieces, smaller skirt over large , then top with bodice piece. Adjust so 2" peeks on each tier. Using threaded needle, join sleeves and top of body.

Assembly

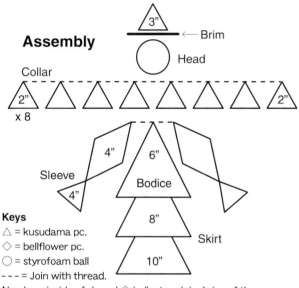

Keys
△ = kusudama pc.
◇ = bellflower pc.
◯ = styrofoam ball
– – – = Join with thread.

Numbers inside of △ and ◇ indicate original size of the paper to be folded.

LIFE SIZE PATTERN

Hat

Crown attaching position

Laminate 2 layers.

❸ Make collar by joining 8 pieces in the round. Apply a dab of glue to top of body, and put collar on it.

❹ Make head. Push toothpick into styrofoam ball. Wrap half of head with crepe paper, and glue edges. Insert toothpick into body, and tie a ribbon bow around neck.

❺ Make hat. Cut kusudama piece made from 3" square into half. Glue the pointed half onto hat.

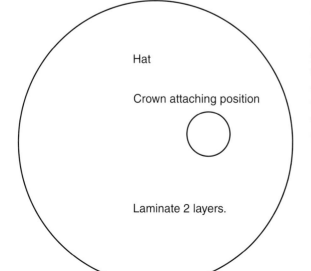

❻ Glue on hat. Glue miniature flowers onto one sleeve to finish.

23. Starlight Princess on page 46

Approximate finished size: 9" W x 9" H
Materials per figure
Prepare [K]usudama pieces referring to pages 2-3.
Prepare [B]ellflower pieces referring to pages 24-25.

1 14" square wrapping paper (silver) for body [K]
2 8" square wrapping paper (silver) for skirt [K]
2 4" square wrapping paper (silver) for sleeves [B]
2 2" square wrapping paper (silver) for collar/skirt [K]
1 6" origami (metallic) for front medallion
2 4" origami (metallic) for back medallions
2 2" origami (metallic) for neck trim
1 2" origami (metallic) for tiara
4" x 6" crepe paper for hair
1 1¼" styrofoam ball for head
1 wooden toothpick

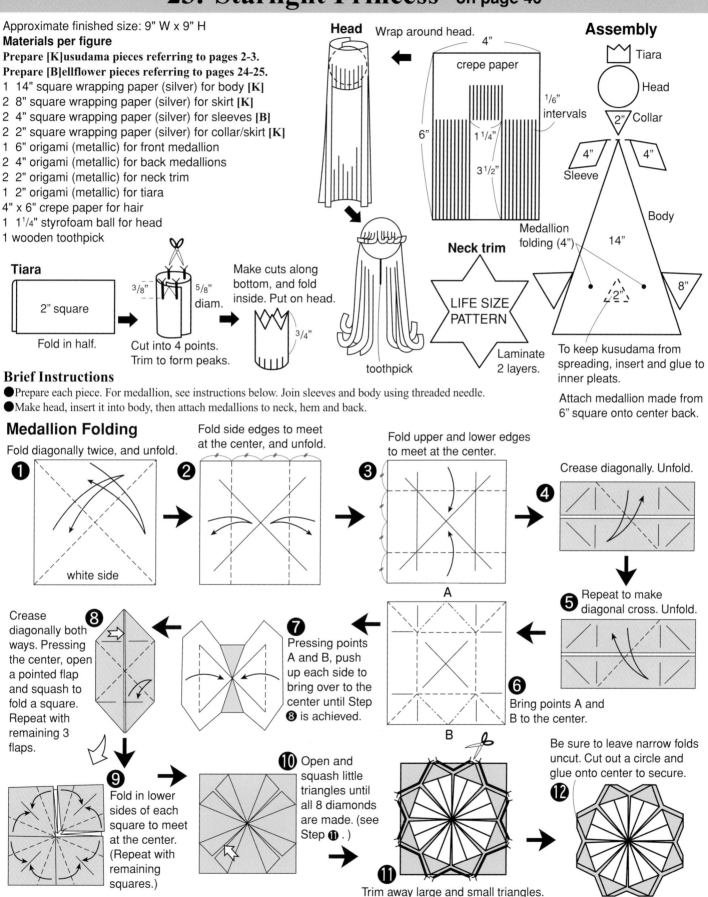

Head Wrap around head.

crepe paper

1/6" intervals

6"   1 1/4"

3 1/2"

Make cuts along bottom, and fold inside. Put on head.

Medallion folding (4")

Neck trim

LIFE SIZE PATTERN

Laminate 2 layers.

toothpick

Assembly

Tiara

Head

2" Collar

4"   4"
Sleeve

14"   Body

2"   8"

To keep kusudama from spreading, insert and glue to inner pleats.

Attach medallion made from 6" square onto center back.

Tiara

2" square

Fold in half.

3/8"   5/8" diam.

Cut into 4 points. Trim to form peaks.

3/4"

Brief Instructions
● Prepare each piece. For medallion, see instructions below. Join sleeves and body using threaded needle.
● Make head, insert it into body, then attach medallions to neck, hem and back.

Medallion Folding

❶ Fold diagonally twice, and unfold.

white side

❷ Fold side edges to meet at the center, and unfold.

❸ Fold upper and lower edges to meet at the center.

A

❹ Crease diagonally. Unfold.

❺ Repeat to make diagonal cross. Unfold.

❻ Bring points A and B to the center.

B

❼ Pressing points A and B, push up each side to bring over to the center until Step ❽ is achieved.

❽ Crease diagonally both ways. Pressing the center, open a pointed flap and squash to fold a square. Repeat with remaining 3 flaps.

❾ Fold in lower sides of each square to meet at the center. (Repeat with remaining squares.)

❿ Open and squash little triangles until all 8 diamonds are made. (see Step ⓫.)

⓫ Trim away large and small triangles.

⓬ Be sure to leave narrow folds uncut. Cut out a circle and glue onto center to secure.

45

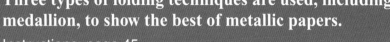

23 Starlight Princess

Three types of folding techniques are used, including medallion, to show the best of metallic papers.

Instructions: page 45

Side View

Rear View

24 Crane Fairy

Sheer yet crisp white dress adorned with delicate little cranes.

Instructions: page 48

Close-up

27. Crane Fairy on page 47

Approximate finished size: 9" W x 14" H

Materials

Prepare [K]usudama pieces referring to pages 2-3.

- 1 21" square tracing paper for body [K]
- 2 4" square tracing paper for sleeves [K]
- 11 3" square tracing paper for collar/sleeves/crown [K]
- 9 2" square tracing paper for brim [K]
- 4 4" square tracing paper for cranes
- 4 3" square tracing paper for cranes
- 1 1¼" styrofoam ball for head
- 3½" x 2½" tracing paper for hair
- ¼" star sequins, Bamboo skewer

Brief Instructions

● Using threaded needle, join 8 kusudama pieces for collar in the round. Place it on pointed top of body.

● Make hair with tracing paper as illustrated, and glue onto head. Push bamboo skewer into styrofoam ball, and insert the other end of skewer into body.

● Join 9 brim pieces in the round. Place it on head, and top with crown piece.

● Make tiered sleeves, and glue under collar.

● Referring to illustrations below, fold 8l cranes. Attach them on skirt hem, by gluing tips of crane wings.

How to attach cranes to front and back skirt hems

● Make 1½" deep cut on center front and center back, along thicker mountain fold. Trim away half of inner flap, and glue remainders.

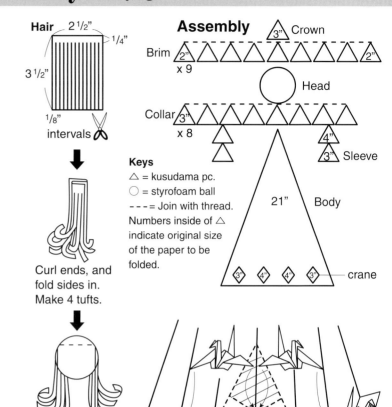

Hair

Curl ends, and fold sides in. Make 4 tufts.

Glue tufts to sides and back of head.

Keys

△ = kusudama pc.
○ = styrofoam ball
- - - = Join with thread.
Numbers inside of △ indicate original size of the paper to be folded.

Assembly — Crown, Brim x 9, Head, Collar x 8, Sleeve, Body, crane

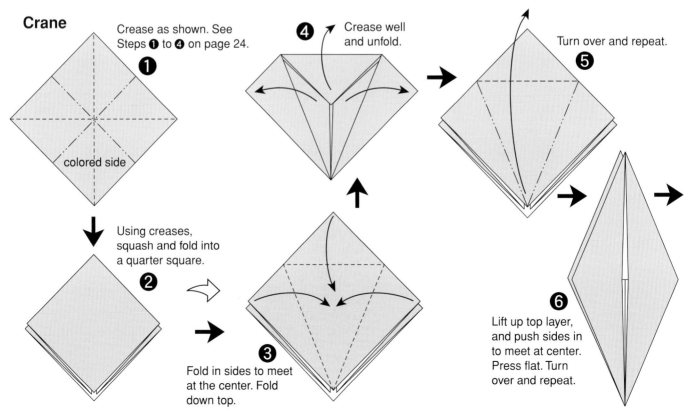

Crane

❶ Crease as shown. See Steps ❶ to ❹ on page 24.

colored side

❷ Using creases, squash and fold into a quarter square.

❸ Fold in sides to meet at the center. Fold down top.

❹ Crease well and unfold.

❺ Turn over and repeat.

❻ Lift up top layer, and push sides in to meet at center. Press flat. Turn over and repeat.

Brief Instructions

● Finish edges of bodice kusudama by folding inside: Pinch a pleat, press down tip triangle, and crease well.

● Make hair. Using threaded needle, join 8 pieces including 3 bang pieces. Glue this circle onto head. Cover top with 2 smaller pieces for front, 4 pieces for back, using glue. Attach florets and pearl bead earrings.

● Pierce craft wire through skirt, bodice to head. Secure with glue.

● Glue on kusudama ruffles all around neckline. Insert tips into pleats. Add 2 extra frills to front.

● Glue on sleeve pieces under the ruffles. Insert pipe cleaners to form arms.

● Attach skirt ruffles. Begin with the lowest ruffles, and add middle ruffles over them.

● Wrap sash around waist and add bow, as illustrated below.

● Attach top ruffles to front skirt.

● Cross arms, and let them hold bouquet.

● With 5-6 pearl beads, make necklace and glue on.

✳ Use glue gun to make works easy.

Approximate finished size: 9" W x 16" H

Materials

Prepare [K]usudama pieces referring to pages 2-3.

1 21" square wax paper (green) for skirt [K]
9 8" square wax paper (green) for bodice/ruffles [K]
8 5" square wax paper (green) for ruffles [K]
10 3" square wax paper (green) for collar/sleeves [K]
7 2 1/2" square wax paper (green) for neck/ruffles [K]
6 2 1/2" square wax paper (brown) for hair [K]
9 2" square wax paper (brown) for hair [K]
7" x 9" wax paper (green) for sash [K]
1 1 1/2" styrofoam ball for head
8 5mm pearl beads
2 6" L pipe cleaners (white)
14" L 1/4" white craft wire
Miniature florets, Miniature bouquet

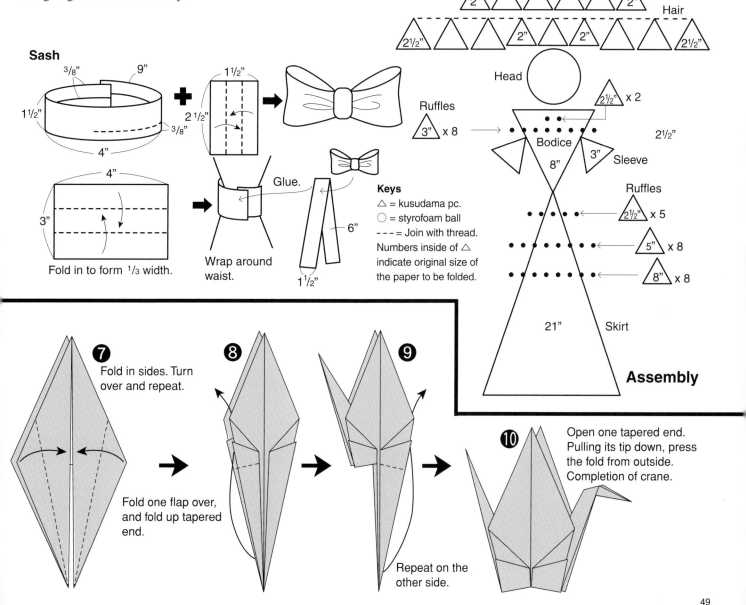

Sash

3/8"   9"
1 1/2"
3/8"
4"

+

1 1/2"
2 1/2"

4"
3"
Fold in to form 1/3 width.

Glue.

Wrap around waist.

6"

1 1/2"

Keys

△ = kusudama pc.
○ = styrofoam ball
- - - = Join with thread.
Numbers inside of △ indicate original size of the paper to be folded.

Hair

2"   2"
2 1/2"   2"   2"   2 1/2"

Head

2 1/2" x 2

Ruffles
3" x 8

Bodice
8"

2 1/2"

3" Sleeve

Ruffles
2 1/2" x 5
5" x 8
8" x 8

21"   Skirt

Assembly

❼ Fold in sides. Turn over and repeat.

Fold one flap over, and fold up tapered end.

❽

❾ Repeat on the other side.

❿ Open one tapered end. Pulling its tip down, press the fold from outside. Completion of crane.

49

25 Miss Caroline

Reminiscent of the days gone by, this ruffled dress appeals its color with wax paper.

Instructions: page 49

Rear View

26 Afternoon Tea

An ideal doll to show the best of vintage papers.

Instructions: page 52

Rear View

26. Afternoon Tea on page 51

Approximate finished size: 6" W x 10" H

Materials

Prepare [K]usudama pieces referring to pages 2-3.

Prepare [B]ellflower pieces referring to pages 24-25.

1 16" square wrapping paper (floral) for body **[K]**
5 4" square wrapping paper (floral) for skirt trim **[K]**
2 4" square wrapping paper (gold) for sleeves **[K]**
9 3" square wrapping paper (gold) for collar **[K]**
2 6" square wrapping paper (floral) for puff sleeves **[B]**
2 each 3" square wrapping paper, floral and gold
1 1¼" styrofoam ball for head
2½" x 6" crepe paper (orange) for hair
2 4" L ¼" cotton cords for arms
2 4" L #20 wrapped wire (white)
2' L ½" ribbon (gold)
1' L ⅝" ribbon (white)
Miniature florets, Bamboo skewer, Board

Keys

△ = kusudama pc.
◇ = bellflower pc.
○ = styrofoam ball
- - - = Join with thread.
Numbers inside of △ and ◇ indicate
original size of the paper to be folded.

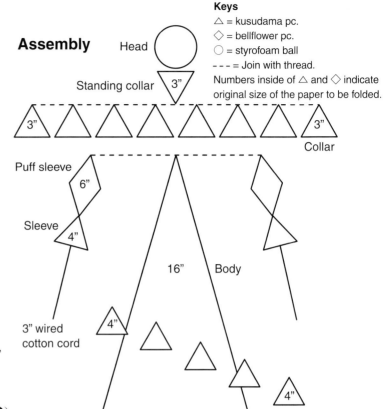

Brief Instructions

● Using threaded needle, join all collar pieces in the round.
● Make arms by threading wire through cotton cord.
● Make sleeves by inserting kusudama piece into bellflower piece, and glue to secure.
● Prepare head as shown below.
● Using threaded needle, join sleeves and body. Place collar on it.
● Place kusudama standing collar, narrow edges down (see Step ❹). Insert head.
● Shape arms to hold the hat. Attach skirt trims with glue.

❶ Join 8 kusudama pieces for collar. Make sleeves by inserting kusudama into bellflower.

❷ Join sleeves with body with thread. Tie loosely.

❸ Place collar on top.

❹ Cut ½" from pointed end of remaining collar piece. Place this on collar, upside down to form a standing collar.

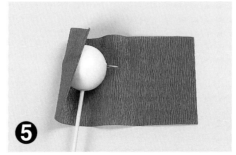

❺ Push bamboo skewer into styrofoam ball. Place a line of glue around the middle of ball, and wrap with crepe paper.

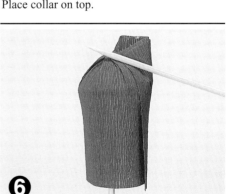

❻ Spread glue over inside of crepe paper. Rolling a thin rod, press down paper, making even folds.

27. Evening Gown on page 54

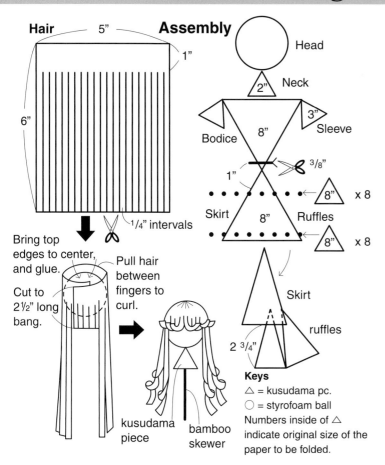

Hair
5"
1"
6"

Assembly

Head

Neck
2"

Bodice
8"

Sleeve
3"

1"
3/8"

8" x 8

Skirt
8"
Ruffles

8" x 8

Skirt

ruffles
2 3/4"

Bring top edges to center, and glue.

Pull hair between fingers to curl.

Cut to 2½" long bang.

1/4" intervals

kusudama piece

bamboo skewer

Keys
△ = kusudama pc.
○ = styrofoam ball
Numbers inside of △ indicate original size of the paper to be folded.

Approximate finished size: 9" W x 10" H

Materials

Prepare [K]usudama pieces referring to pages 2-3.

18 8" square wrapping paper (floral) for bodice/skirt/ruffles [K]
 2 3" square wrapping paper (floral) for sleeves [K]
 1 2" square tracing paper for neck [K]
1 1¼" styrofoam ball for head
6" x 5" crepe paper for hair
2 5" fine pipe cleaners for arms
Miniature bouquet, Bamboo skewer

Brief Instructions

● Finish edges of bodice kusudama by folding inside: Pinch a pleat, press down tip triangle, and crease well.

● In this doll, tiers of ruffles support the "short skirt." Glue bottom tier to inside of skirt hem at a slant so about 3" of the tier shows.

● Trim away 3/8" from pointed tip of bodice, and set on skirt. Glue to secure.

● Glue on upper tier of ruffles 1" below the waist.

● Attach sleeves to sides. Insert pipe cleaners into sleeves, and glue to secure.

● Make head as illustrated. Push in bamboo skewer, and insert into bodice together with neck piece.

● Shape arms and let them hold the bouquet.

Hat

Cut out circles.

Put on ring.

1½"

2"
Crown

Join and glue ends of ¼" wide strip.

Brim floral pattern

3"
2½"

Laminate board with 2 sheets of gold paper.

floral pattern

gold

board

Fold back edges of crown, and glue onto brim.

Wrap with ribbon and tie a bow.

Fold ribbon in half. Wrap around crown.

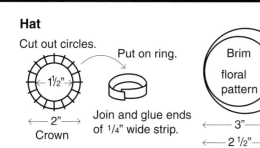

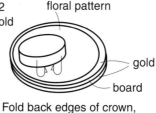

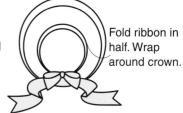

❼

Cut into hair in the same manner as above. Using a toothpick or thin rod, curl each end.

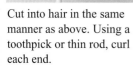

❽

Insert white wrapped wire into cotton cord. Make 2.

Insert and glue arms. Tie the narrow ribbon around neck and make a bow.

Make hat as shown above, and let the arms hold it. Glue kusudama ornaments onto the skirt.

❾

❿

27 Evening Gown

The triangular bodice is a kusudama piece set upside down. Note the folded neckline.

Instructions: page 53

Rear View

28 Picnic Outing

As fresh as sprouting leaves, green wax paper creates a special effect.

Instructions: page 56

28. Picnic Outing　on page 55

Approximate finished size: 10" W x 11" H
Materials
Prepare [K]usudama pieces referring to pages 2-3.
1 14" square wax paper (green) for body **[K]**
8 8" square wax paper (green) for ruffles **[K]**
10 5" square wax paper (green) for ruffles/hat **[K]**
20 3" square wax paper (green) for collar/sleeves/ruffles/hat **[K]**
7 2" square wax paper (green) for hat/sleeves **[K]**
1 2¹/₂" styrofoam ball for head
Doll hair
Cotton jersey (skin color) for head
Nylon lining (dark brown) for eyes
Miniature florets
6" L ¹/₁₆" craft wire, cut in half
9" L #18 wrapped wire
3" basket with handle, Miniature bouquet
Polyfil

Brief Instructions
●Prepare hat and collar. Using threaded needle, join hat pieces in the round. Join collar pieces as well.
●Place collar on body. Make head as shown right, push wrapped wire into it, and insert into collar/body.
●Make sleeves by combining 2 pieces of different sizes. Glue onto collar. Bend craft wire into an oval hook, and insert into sleeves with glue.
●Attach ruffles beginning with the bottom tier, carefully checking balance. Attach middle tier, then top tier.
●Hang basket filled with bouquet.

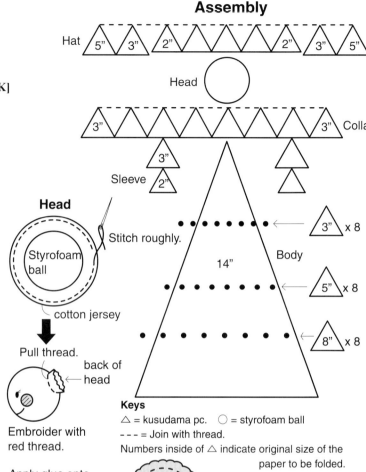

Assembly

Hat

Head

Collar

Sleeve

Head

Styrofoam ball

cotton jersey

Stitch roughly.

Pull thread.

back of head

Embroider with red thread.

3" x 8
5" x 8
8" x 8
Body
14"

Keys
△ = kusudama pc.　◯ = styrofoam ball
- - - = Join with thread.
Numbers inside of △ indicate original size of the paper to be folded.

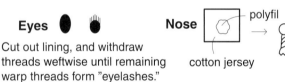

Eyes ● ᷤ

Cut out lining, and withdraw threads weftwise until remaining warp threads form "eyelashes."

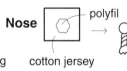

Nose　polyfil

cotton jersey

Apply glue onto wrong side, and squeeze tightly. Trim off twist when dry.

Glue on doll hair.

30. Little Duchess　on page 59

Approximate finished size: 14" W x 15" H
Materials
Prepare [K]usudama pieces referring to pages 2-3.
3 21" square wrapping paper for body **[K]**
8 5" square wrapping paper for collar **[K]**
13 4" square wrapping paper for hat/sleeves **[K]**
1 1¹/₂" styrofoam ball for head
Doll hair
Knitted fabric for face
Felt (black, red)
18" L 1¹/₂" cotton lace edging
2' L ¹/₈" ribbon, cut into quarters
1' L ¹/₄" ribbon for hair
2'6" x 8" pearly tulle netting
Miniature florets, Bamboo skewer

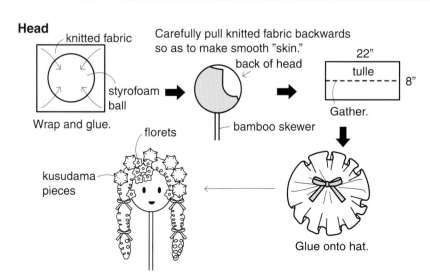

Head　knitted fabric

styrofoam ball

Wrap and glue.

Carefully pull knitted fabric backwards so as to make smooth "skin."

back of head

bamboo skewer

22"
tulle
8"
Gather.

Glue onto hat.

florets

kusudama pieces

29. Ball Gown on page 58

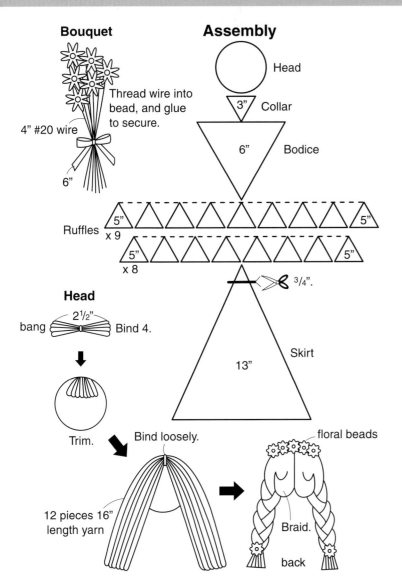

Bouquet

Thread wire into bead, and glue to secure.

4" #20 wire

6"

Assembly

Head

Collar 3"

Bodice 6"

Ruffles x 9 — 5" ... 5"

x 8 — 5" ... 5"

3/4".

Skirt 13"

Head

bang 2 1/2" Bind 4.

Trim.

Bind loosely.

12 pieces 16" length yarn

floral beads

Braid.

back

Approximate finished size: 8" W x 11" H
Materials
Prepare [K]usudama pieces referring to pages 2 -3.
- 1 13 " square construction paper for skirt [K]
- 1 6" square construction paper for bodice [K]
- 17 5 " square tracing paper for ruffles [K]
- 1 3" square tracing paper for collar [K]
- 1 11" diameter tracing paper for overskirt
- 1 5" diameter tracing paper for bodice overlay
- 1 1 1/2" styrofoam ball for head
- Chunky knitting yarn for hair
- 1' L 1/8" matching color ribbon, cut into halves
- 32 matching color floral beads
- 9" L 1/3" thick wrapped wire, cut into halves for arms
- 6 4" L #20 wrapped wire for bouquet
- Bamboo skewer

Brief Instructions
● Prepare overlays by trimming edges with pinking shears. Lay over skirt and bodice paper, and glue at several points. Fold 2 layers together into each kusudama piece.
● Trim away pointed tip of skirt piece, and insert bodice piece into the hole just made.
● Using threaded needle, join 9 ruffle pieces for upper tier, 8 pieces for lower tier. Wrap around waist and knot, adjusting tightness.
● Insert collar into bodice. Make head with bamboo skewer and insert into collar.
● Attach floral beads to centers of ruffle pieces and skirt hem using glue.
● Attach arms of thick wrapped wire by gluing behind side pleats.
● Make a bow with ribbon. Glue floral bead onto collar.
● Make bouquet by inserting wire into floral beads as illustrated, and glue onto hand.

Hat 4" ... 4"

Head

Collar 5" ... 5"

4"

Sleeve 4"

Assembly

Body 21"

Brief Instructions
● Join 3 body pieces. Place 2 pieces facing you.
● Prepare hat and collar by joining each in the round.
● Prepare head as illustrated on the opposite page. Glue on doll hair. Decorate hair with tiny kusudama pieces, florets and ribbon bows. Cut eyes and mouth out of felt, and glue onto face. Attach floret "earrings."
● Onto body, place collar and gathered tulle netting. Insert bamboo skewer of head into body, and glue to secure.
● Join 2 sleeve pieces, and attach underneath the collar. Repeat with other side. Make a bouquet by wrapping florets with 8" square tulle netting, and glue onto dress.

Keys
△ = kusudama pc. ○ = styrofoam ball - - - = Join with thread.
Numbers inside of △ indicate original size of the paper to be folded.

57

29 Ball Gown

"Organza" overlay and ruffles give
this dress a fresh look.

Instructions: page 57

Rear View

30 Little Duchess

This lovely wide dress consists of only three kusudama pieces.

Instructions: page 56

31. Parasol Princess on page 62

Approximate finished size: 10" W x 15" H

Materials

Prepare [K]usudama pieces referring to pages 2-3.

Prepare [B]ellflower pieces referring to pages 24-25.

1 16" square tracing paper (pink) for skirt [K]

1 12" square tracing paper (blue) for skirt [K]

4 8" square tracing paper(blue) for bodice/ruffles [K]

3 8" square tracing paper(pink) for ruffles [K]

2 8" square tracing paper (blue) for skirt trim[B]

2 5" square tracing paper (pink) for sleeves[B]

1 8" square tracing paper (pink) for parasol

1 5" square tracing paper (white) for parasol

1 5" square tracing paper (pink) for collar

1 1¹/₂" styrofoam ball for head

5¹/₂" x 6" crepe paper for hair

14" and 7" L #18 wrapped wire

Brief Instructions

● Stack 2 skirt pieces and glue to secure.

● Using threaded wire, join 6 pieces for ruffles in the round. Knot and wrap around skirt.

● Place joined sleeves on bodice piece.

● Make collar referring to illustrations at the bottom of the opposite page. Place on bodice.

● Make head as illustrated, and push in 14" wrapped wire. Insert into bodice.

● Make parasol and collar as illustrated below. Make slits into sides of collar, and pierce parasol wire through one slit into bodice. Bend end into hook, and glue to secure.

● Glue on skirt trims of bellflower pieces.

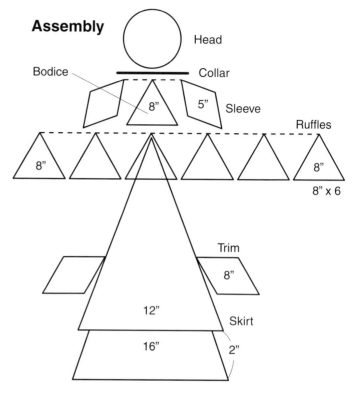

Assembly

Head

Bodice — Collar

8" 5" Sleeve

Ruffles

8" 8" 8" x 6

Trim

8"

12" Skirt

16" 2"

Keys

△ = kusudama pc.   ◇ = bellflower pc.

◯ = styrofoam ball   - - - = Join with thread.

Numbers inside of △ and ◇ indicate original size of the paper to be folded.

Umbrella

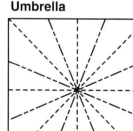

For creasing into 16 equal parts, work 8" pink and 5" white papers in the same manner as page 2 until Step ➒. (Umbrella fold.)

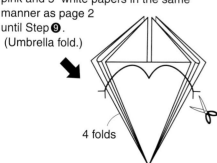

4 folds

Layer with outer parasol (pink).

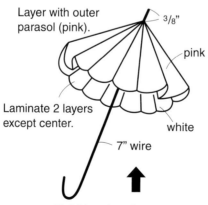

3/8"

pink

Laminate 2 layers except center.

white

7" wire

Unfold and push up center from back so it raises. Turn over.

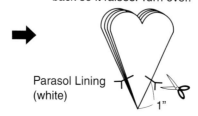

Parasol Lining (white)

1"

Hair

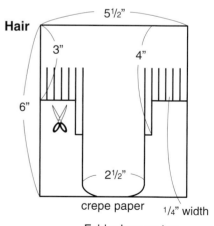

5¹/₂"

3" 4"

6"

2¹/₂"

crepe paper   ¹/₄" width

Fold edges on top.

Head

60

32. Sheer Fantasy on page 63

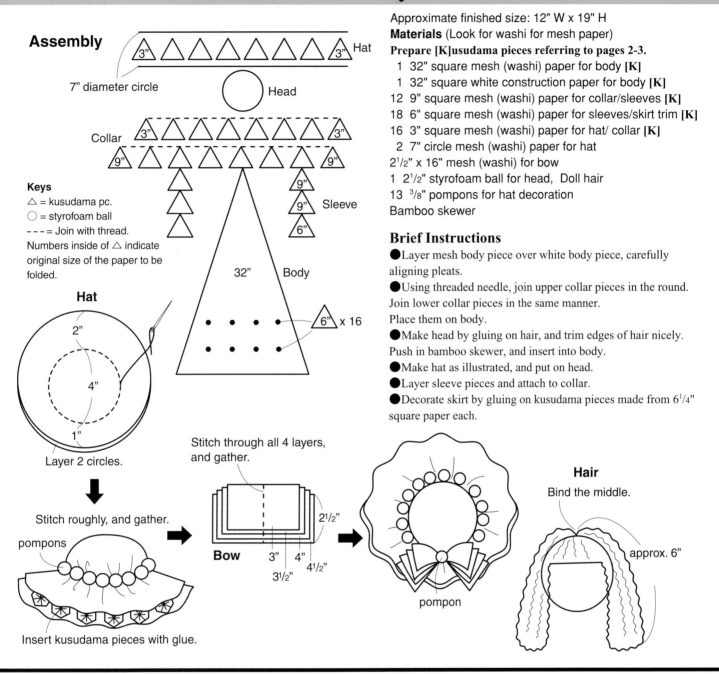

Assembly

7" diameter circle

Hat

Head

Collar

Keys
△ = kusudama pc.
○ = styrofoam ball
- - - = Join with thread.
Numbers inside of △ indicate original size of the paper to be folded.

Hat

2"

4"

1"

Layer 2 circles.

Sleeve

32" Body

6" x 16

Stitch roughly, and gather.

pompons

Insert kusudama pieces with glue.

Stitch through all 4 layers, and gather.

Bow

2½"

3" 4"

3½" 4½"

pompon

Hair

Bind the middle.

approx. 6"

Approximate finished size: 12" W x 19" H
Materials (Look for washi for mesh paper)
Prepare [K]usudama pieces referring to pages 2-3.
  1 32" square mesh (washi) paper for body [K]
  1 32" square white construction paper for body [K]
12 9" square mesh (washi) paper for collar/sleeves [K]
18 6" square mesh (washi) paper for sleeves/skirt trim [K]
16 3" square mesh (washi) paper for hat/ collar [K]
  2 7" circle mesh (washi) paper for hat
2½" x 16" mesh (washi) for bow
1 2½" styrofoam ball for head, Doll hair
13 ⅜" pompons for hat decoration
Bamboo skewer

Brief Instructions
●Layer mesh body piece over white body piece, carefully aligning pleats.
●Using threaded needle, join upper collar pieces in the round. Join lower collar pieces in the same manner.
Place them on body.
●Make head by gluing on hair, and trim edges of hair nicely. Push in bamboo skewer, and insert into body.
●Make hat as illustrated, and put on head.
●Layer sleeve pieces and attach to collar.
●Decorate skirt by gluing on kusudama pieces made from 6¼" square paper each.

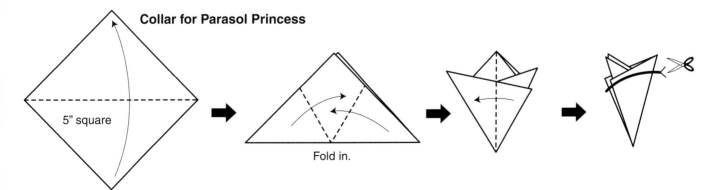

Collar for Parasol Princess

5" square

Fold in.

31 Parasol Princess

Elegant organza image is recreated with pastel tone tracing paper.

Instructions: page 60

Rear View

32 Sheer Fantasy

Mesh paper made of washi is sturdier than it looks. An elegant doll of 19" height.

Instructions: page 61

Approximate finished size: 10" W x 18" H
Materials
Prepare [K]usudama pieces referring to pages 2-3.
18 9" square mesh (washi) paper for bodice/skirt [K]
18 9" square tracing paper for bodice/skirt [K]
6 3" square mesh (washi) paper for hat/sleeves [K]
6 3" square tracing paper for hat/sleeves [K]
4 2" square mesh (washi) paper for hat [K]
4 2" square tracing paper for hat [K]
1 1 1/2" square mesh (washi) paper for collar [K]
1 1 1/2" square tracing paper for collar [K]
1 1 1/2" styrofoam ball for head
Doll hair
12" square cotton jersey for face
Nylon lining for eyes, Paper clay
8" x 5" oval wooden board for base
2' 3/4" organza ribbon for bouquet
Miniature bouquet, Miniature florets
1' L 1/6" thick wrapped wire, cut in half
2' L 1/3" thick wrapped wire for legs
8" #18 wrapped wire, Polyfil

Assembly

Keys
△ = kusudama pc.
○ = styrofoam ball
- - - - = Join with thread.
Numbers inside or outside of △
indicate original size of the paper
to be folded.

Wire structure

Head
Stitch roughly.
Pull thread.
back of head
doll hair
styrofoam ball
cotton jersey

Nose
polyfil
cotton jersey

Apply glue over wrong side, and squeeze tightly. Trim away twisted part when dry.

Eyes
Cut out lining, and withdraw threads weftwise until remaining warp threads form "eyelashes."

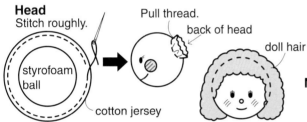

Approximate finished size: 12" W x 19" H
Materials
Prepare [K]usudama pieces referring to pages 2-3.
18 9" square mesh (washi) paper for bodice/skirt [K]
18 9" square tracing paper for bodice/skirt [K]
6 3" square mesh (washi) paper for hat/sleeves [K]
6 3" square tracing paper for hat/sleeves [K]
4 2" square mesh (washi) paper for hat [K]
4 2" square tracing paper for hat [K]
1 1 1/2" square mesh (washi) paper for collar [K]
1 1 1/2" square tracing paper for collar [K]
1 1 1/2" styrofoam ball for head
Doll hair, 12" square cotton jersey for face
Nylon lining for eyes, Paper clay
8" x 5" oval wooden board for base
Miniature bouquet, Miniature florets
8 5mm pearl beads for headpiece
8" x 3/4" mesh (washi) paper for bow
6" x 2" mesh (washi) paper for bow
20" x 2 3/4" mesh (washi) paper for waist
1' L 1/6" thick wrapped wire for arms
27" L 1/3" thick wrapped wire for legs
8" #18 wrapped wire, Polyfil

Brief Instructions for #33 and #34
● For all kusudama pieces, layer mesh and tracing paper of the same size, and fold together.
● Make legs by wrapping thick wrapped wire with cotton jersey. Glue ends.
● Fold thickest wire at the middle. Twist #18 wire around the bend, and insert into skirt base. Using threaded needle, join kusudama pieces for skirt tiers. Put tiers through skirt base, then put bodice on.
● To #33, glue miniature florets, and to #34, glue gathered mesh of 20"x 3" size around waist.
● Finish neckline by folding in triangular edges. Make head and insert into body.
● Form shoe shapes with paper clay, and thrust legs or wire into them. When clay is dry, cover with florets using glue.
● Glue sleeves onto bodice. Cut arm wire into halves, and insert each into sleeve. Secure with glue and let arms hold the bouquet.
● To #33, glue on hat made of joined 8 kusudama pieces. To #34, glue on kusudama pieces and bows.
● Make features as illustrated. For #34, draw eyes, mouth and cheeks with permanent markers.

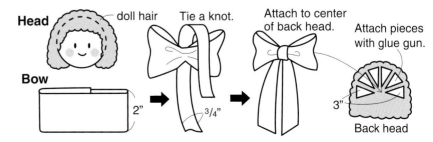

36. Flower Girls on page 70

Cape

Cut 4" paper doily in half.

10"   Cut off. ✂

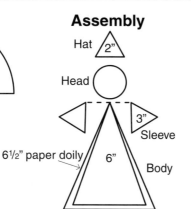

Keys

△ = kusudama pc. ○ = styrofoam ball

- - - = Join with thread.

Numbers inside of △ indicate original size of the paper to be folded.

Assembly

Hat   2"

Head

Sleeve   3"

6½" paper doily   6"   Body

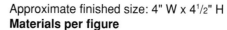

Approximate finished size: 4" W x 4½" H

Materials per figure

Prepare [K]usudama pieces referring to pages 2-3.

1 2" square construction paper for hat **[K]**

2 3" square construction paper for sleeves **[K]**

1 6" square construction paper for body **[K]**

1 6½" paper doily for overskirt

1 4" paper doily cut in half for cape

1 ¾" styrofoam ball for head

2" x 4" crepe paper for hair

10" L ½" organza ribbon for head

2½" L pipe cleaner (pink) for arms

Wooden toothpick, Miniature floret

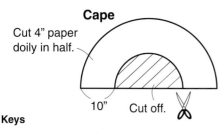

❶ Fold larger paper doily in half. Repeat 3 times until 16 sections are made. Unfold and fold again alternating mountain and valley fold to resemble an umbrella.

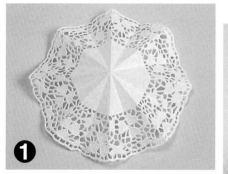

❷ With this doily, cover body made of largest construction paper, aligning pleats. Secure top by applying glue only to valley folds.

Using threaded needle, join sleeve, body and sleeve. Tie ends of thread loosely. **❸**

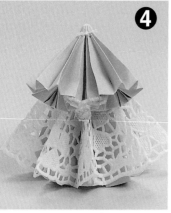

❹ Twist the middle of pipe cleaner into a loop to form hands, and insert ends into sleeves.

Cut cape from paper doily. Wrap shoulders with cape, and glue ends.

❺

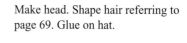

Make head. Shape hair referring to page 69. Glue on hat. **❻**

❼ Make a bow with ribbon, and glue onto back of hat.

❽ Apply glue onto top of body, and insert head into it.

To finish, insert stem of floret into the loop of pipe cleaner. **❾**

33 Dorothy

Mesh washi and tracing paper are layered and folded together to hold the shape.

Instructions: page 64

Side View

34 Ballerina

Bowing dancer with legs made of thick wrapped wire for stabilization.

Instructions: page 64

35. Tiered Lace Gown on page 70

Approximate finished size: 4¹/₂" W x 9" H

Materials

Prepare [K]usudama pieces referring to pages 2-3.

10 2" square construction paper for hat/collar **[K]**

 2 4" square construction paper for sleeves **[K]**

 3 8" square construction paper for dress **[K]**

 3 8" paper doilies for dress

2¹/₂" x 4" crepe paper for hair

12" x 8" tulle netting

1 1" styrofoam ball for head

Wooden toothpick, Floral tape (white)

2 10" L #22 wrapped wire

1 2" L #28 wrapped wire

Miniature florets, Sequins

Assembly

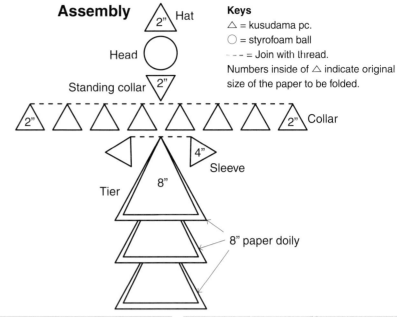

Keys

△ = kusudama pc.

○ = styrofoam ball

- - - = Join with thread.

Numbers inside of △ indicate original size of the paper to be folded.

Hat 2"

Head

Standing collar 2"

Collar 2" ... 2"

Sleeve 4"

Tier 8"

8" paper doily

❶ Fold larger paper doily in half. Repeat 3 times until 16 sections are made. Unfold and fold again, alternating mountain and valley fold to resemble an umbrella.

❷ With this doily, cover a tier made of construction paper, aligning pleats. Secure top by applying glue only to valley folds.

❸ In the same manner, make 2 more sets of tiers. Join all tiers, carefully aligning pleats so as not to damage the lace pattern.

❹ After aligning all pleats, set each tier 1¹/₂" apart and glue to secure.

❺ Using threaded needle, join sleeve, body, then sleeve, and tie with some ease.

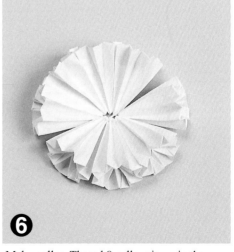

❻ Make collar. Thread 8 collar pieces in the round. Pulling thread tightly, tie a knot.

7

Apply glue onto top of body, and put on collar.

8

Make head. Push toothpick into styrofoam ball. Make deep cuts into long edge of crepe paper. Apply glue onto backside of top edges, and glue onto head.

9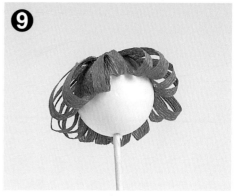

Bring up hair and glue at top.

10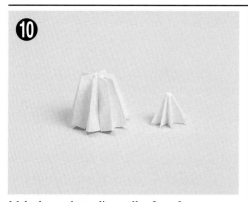

Make hat and standing collar from 2 kusudama pieces. Trim away pointed tip from each piece, and save one for hat. For collar, glue together pleats on cut edges.

11

Squeeze edges of tulle into top hole of hat, and glue to secure. Decorate by gluing sequins.

12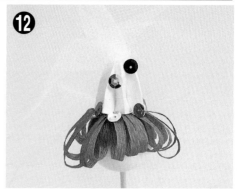

Apply glue onto head, and put on hat.

13

Apply glue onto center of collar, and place standing collar. Insert toothpick of head through collars into body.

14

Make arms. Bend 10" wire. Wrap each with white floral tape, and insert into each sleeve. Glue to secure.

15

Cross ends of arms, and attach bouquet tied up with ribbon with #28 wire.

BRIDAL PARTY

35 Tiered Lace Gown

**Happy bride accompanied by flower girls.
Delicately patterned paper doilies construct a lean,
tiered dress with contrasting solid paper underdress.**

Instructions: page 68

36 Flower Girls

Instructions: page 65

37 Bridal Gown with Train

Fold circular paper doilies using "Umbrella" folding technique as well as Tiered Lace Gown on the opposite page.

Instructions: page 72

37. Bridal Gown with Train on page 71

Approximate finished size: 8" W x 8" H

Materials

Prepare [K]usudama pieces referring to pages 2-3.

9 2" square construction paper for collar[K]
3 5" square construction paper for sleeves/bodice[K]
2 9" square construction paper for skirt[K]
2 9" paper doilies for skirt
3 4" paper doily for sleeves
1¹/₂" x 3" crepe paper for hair
40" and 12"L ¹/₄" ribbon (silver)
1 1" styrofoam ball for head

Wooden toothpick, Floral tape (white)
2 10" L #22 wrapped wire
1 2" L #28 wrapped wire, Miniature florets

Keys

△ = kusudama pc.
○ = styrofoam ball
- - - = Join with thread.
Numbers inside of △
indicate original size of the
paper to be folded.

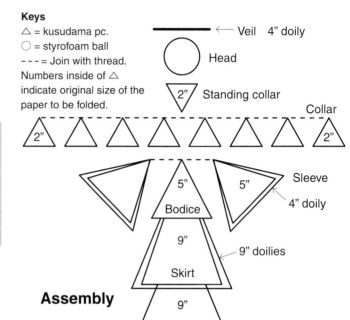

← Veil   4" doily

Head

2" Standing collar

Collar

2" 2"

5" 5" Sleeve

4" doily

Bodice

9" 9" doilies

Skirt

9"

Assembly

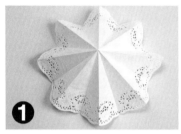

❶ Fold larger paper doily in half. Repeat 3 times until 16 sections are made. Unfold and fold again alternating mountain and valley fold to resemble an umbrella.

❷ Layer half of another doily and glue along edges of upper layer only. Crease upper, layered section according to the lower layer to make skirt.

❸ Join 2 kusudama pieces made from 9" squares. Align pleats carefully, and glue 1¹/₂" apart.

❹ Cover skirt with layered doilies. Align pleats and glue valley folds to secure.

❺ Stack on bodice piece carefully so as not to damage the lace pattern. Glue to secure.

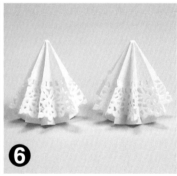

❻ Make sleeves. Cover kusudama piece with paper doily folded in the same manner as Step ❶.

❼ Using threaded needle, join sleeves with top of bodice. Tie ends loosely.

❽ Join 8 collar pieces in the round. Apply glue and place it on top of bodice with glue.

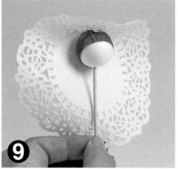

❾ Make head. Push toothpick into styrofoam ball. Wrap half of head with crepe paper, and glue top edges. Glue on 4" doily.

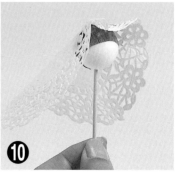

❿ Pressing top and sides of lace edges, glue as shown.

38. Blooming Gown on page 74

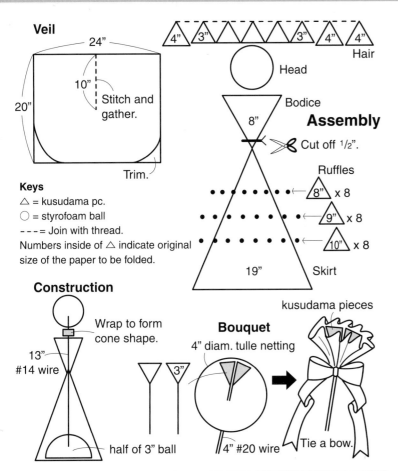

Veil

24"

10"

20"

Stitch and gather.

Trim.

Keys

△ = kusudama pc.

◯ = styrofoam ball

- - - - = Join with thread.

Numbers inside of △ indicate original size of the paper to be folded.

Hair

4" 3" 3" 4" 4"

Head

Bodice

8"

Cut off ½".

Assembly

Ruffles

8" x 8

9" x 8

10" x 8

19" Skirt

Construction

Wrap to form cone shape.

13" #14 wire

half of 3" ball

Bouquet

kusudama pieces

4" diam. tulle netting

3"

4" #20 wire

Tie a bow.

Approximate finished size: 11" W x 15" H

Materials

Prepare [K]usudama pieces referring to pages 2-3.

1 19" square tracing paper for skirt [K]

8 10" square tracing paper for ruffles [K]

8 9" square tracing paper for ruffles [K]

9 8" square tracing paper for ruffles [K]

3 4" square tracing paper for hair [K]

7 3" square tracing paper for hair/bouquet [K]

2 2" x 6" tracing paper for arms

22" x 24" and 4" diam. lame tulle for veil/bouquet

1 2" styrofoam ball for head

1 3" styrofoam ball cut in half for base

2'8" L 1" ribbon, Miniature bouquet

2 4" L #20 wrapped wire

1 13" L #14 wrapped wire

Brief Instructions

● Using threaded needle, join 8 pieces for hair. Glue hair to styrofoam ball.

● Make base by pushing in #14 wire into styrofoam hemisphere.

● Pierce wire through skirt and bodice. Glue waist joint.

● Wrap tracing paper around neck forming a cone. Attach head and glue to secure.

● Attach skirt ruffles from bottom. Glue on kusudama pieces around skirt, checking overall balance.

● Insert 6 stems of florets into neck edges.

● Make arms by wrapping #20 wire with 2" wide strip. Cut to 5" length. Make 2.

● Insert arms into sides of bodice and glue to secure. Let them hold bouquet.

● Glue on veil, and decorate with 3 florets.

＊ Use glue gun to make works easy.

⓫ To make standing collar, trim away about ³/₈" from pointed top of kusudama piece. Glue cut edges to maintain shape.

⓬ Holding collar upside down, pass through toothpick of head.

Make arms by folding #22 wire in half, and wrap with floral tape. Make 2. Insert into sleeves and glue. Bend arms to cross, and place bunch of florets.

⓭ Apply glue to center of collar, and insert head.

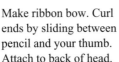

Make ribbon bow. Curl ends by sliding between pencil and your thumb. Attach to back of head.

⓮

⓯

38 Blooming Gown
Luxurious wedding gown accented with innocent marguerites.

Instructions: page 73

Close-up

39 Pearly Gown

Cute tracing paper gown is enhanced with delicate details. Use glue gun for decoration.

Instructions: 76

Close-up

39. Pearly Gown on page 75

Approximate finished size: 14" W x 14" H

Materials

Prepare [K]usudama pieces referring to pages 2-3.

- 1 22" square tracing paper for body [K]
- 8 10" square tracing paper for ruffles [K]
- 8 9" square tracing paper for ruffles [K]
- 2 5" square tracing paper for hat [K]
- 17 4" square tracing paper for hat/collar/sleeves [K]

22" x 40" lame tulle netting
1 2" styrofoam ball for head
1 3" styrofoam ball for base
Doll hair
3mm, 5mm and 8mm pearl beads
5mm teardrop-shape pearl beads
12" L $^1/_8$" bamboo stick
8" L $^1/_{16}$" wrapped wire, cut into halves
Miniature bouquet and florets

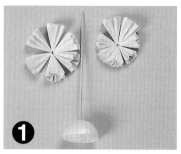

❶ Prepare hat and collar. Using threaded needle, join pieces in the round. Push bamboo stick into base.

❷ Push toothpick into head to make your work easier. Apply glue over head, and attach hat pieces.

❸ Place body, collar and head, by piercing each with bamboo stick set on base. Glue to secure.

❹ Attach ruffle pieces beginning with the lower row.

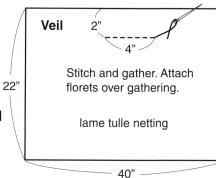

Veil
2"
4"
22"
Stitch and gather. Attach florets over gathering.

lame tulle netting

40"

Hat
5" 4" 4" 5"

Head **Assembly**

Structure

bamboo stick

3" styrofoam ball cut in half

Hand

Wrapped wire

Insert bouquet here.

Keys
△ = kusudama pc.
○ = styrofoam ball
- - - = Join with thread.
Numbers inside of △ indicate original size of the paper to be folded.

Collar 4"

Sleeve 4"

22"

Body

10" x 8
9" x 8

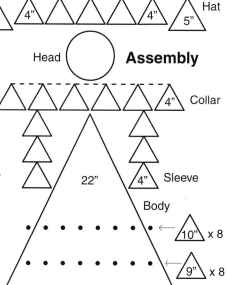

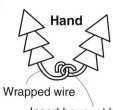

❺ Make sleeves by joining 3 kusudama pieces each. Glue to collar.

Insert 4" wire through each sleeve, and curl ends to let them hold bouquet.

❼ Make necklace by threading pearl beads, and glue. Using glue gun, attach pearl beads generously onto edges of tiers.

Glue on hair under the hat. Attach florets and veil.

76

Approximate finished size: 8" W x 32" H

Materials

Prepare [K]usudama pieces referring to pages 2-3.

 1 14" square plain washi paper for jacket **[K]**
 8 8" square plain washi paper for trousers **[K]**
 2 6" square plain washi paper for sleeves **[K]**
 4 5" square plain washi paper for sleeves **[K]**
10 3" square plain washi paper for hair **[K]**
 1 6" square plain washi paper for hat
 2 2" styrofoam balls for head/shoes
 8" L ⁵/₈" satin ribbon (white)
 6 8mm pearl beads
 2 13"L ¹/₈" wrapped wire
 1 6" L ¹/₈" wrapped wire
 4 miniature florets
 Permanent marker (black)

Brief Instructions

●Make shoes. Cut one styrofoam ball into halves, and color both with permanent marker.

●Push 13" wrapped wire into each shoe. Pierce through 4 trouser pieces each. Adjust the lengths.

●Bend each wire into a crank shape as shown, and secure joint by binding with floral tape or extra wire.

●Join sleeves and body using threaded needle. Set this over the joined wire.

●Using threaded needle, join 10 hair pieces in the round and glue onto head. Make hat and glue onto head.

●Insert head. Wrap neck with ribbon, then attach tie.

●Attach florets to hat and chest. Attach pearl beads to jacket.

41. Slender Gown

on page 78

Brief Instructions

●Prepare hat and collar by joining pieces in the round.

●Place collar on body. Push toothpick into styrofoam head, and insert into collar.

●Glue on hat. Place a kusudama piece on top, and glue to secure. Attach a pompon on tip.

●Insert sleeve pieces into collar.

●Cut out floral lace patterns from lace fabric, and glue onto skirt. Cut out scallop pattern, and glue onto hem.

●Tie a bow around neck. Attach a cascade bouquet to end of one arm.

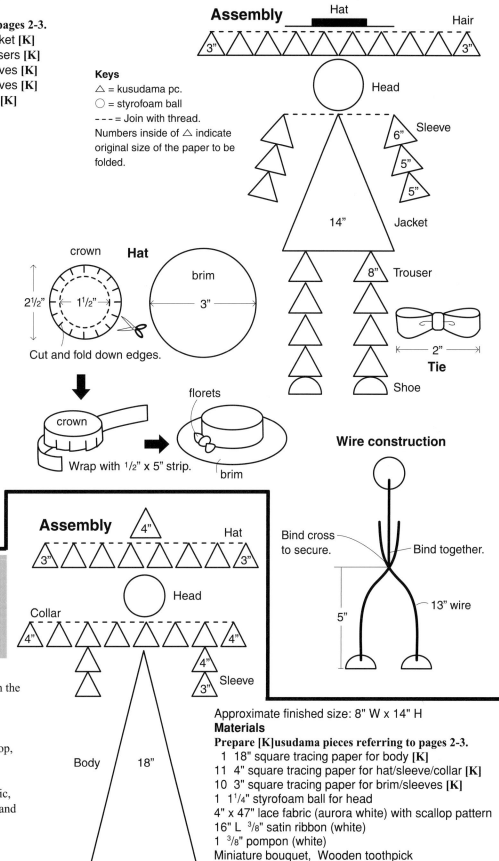

Keys
△ = kusudama pc.
○ = styrofoam ball
- - - = Join with thread.
Numbers inside of △ indicate original size of the paper to be folded.

Hat

crown

brim

2¹/₂"   1¹/₂"   3"

Cut and fold down edges.

crown

Wrap with ¹/₂" x 5" strip.

florets

brim

Assembly (Tuxedo)

Hat   Hair
3"   3"

Head

Sleeve   6"
5"
5"

Jacket   14"

Trouser   8"

Shoe

Tie   2"

Assembly (Slender Gown)

4"

Hat
3"   3"

Head

Collar
4"   4"

4"
3"   Sleeve

Body   18"

Wire construction

Bind cross to secure.   Bind together.

5"   13" wire

Approximate finished size: 8" W x 14" H

Materials

Prepare [K]usudama pieces referring to pages 2-3.

 1 18" square tracing paper for body **[K]**
11 4" square tracing paper for hat/sleeve/collar **[K]**
10 3" square tracing paper for brim/sleeves **[K]**
 1 1¹/₄" styrofoam ball for head
 4" x 47" lace fabric (aurora white) with scallop pattern
16" L ³/₈" satin ribbon (white)
 1 ³/₈" pompon (white)
 Miniature bouquet, Wooden toothpick

40 Tuxedo
Tall yet stable doll in a charming tux.

Instructions: page 77

41 Slender Gown
Sheer tracing paper teamed with delicate lace fabric.

Instructions: page 77

42 White Wedding

Eye-catching doll couple finished with silver glitter.

Instructions: page 80

Rear View of Groom

42. White Wedding on page 79

Bride
Approximate finished size: 14" W x 12" H
Materials
Prepare [K]usudama pieces referring to pages 2-3.
  1 21" square tracing paper for body [K]
  8 11" square tracing paper for ruffles [K]
  8 10" square tracing paper for ruffles [K]
  2 5" square tracing paper for hair [K]
19 4" square tracing paper for hair/collar/sleeves [K]
22" x 24" lame tulle netting, Miniature bouquet
1 2" styrofoam ball for head
1 3" styrofoam ball for base, cut in half
2mm and 8mm pearl beads
11" L #16 wrapped wire, 2 extra-thin marking pins
Glitter glue (lame)

Brief Instructions
● Make base by pushing in wire into halved styrofoam ball.
● Stack on body, and then styrofoam head.
● Using threaded needle, join 7 hair pieces in the round. Place on head and glue to secure.
● Likewise, join collar pieces, and glue to ³/₄" below head.
● Make necklace with 8mm pearl beads, and attach to neck.
● Attach ruffles, beginning with lower tier glued to 1¹/₄" above hem. Attach upper ruffle tier just below collar. Check overall balance.
● Insert sleeves into collar, and glue at an angle.
● Make earrings by pushing thin marking pins into pearl beads, and glue on. Glue on veil made as illustrated. Glue bouquet onto end of one sleeve.
● Apply glitter glue and 2mm beads along edges of kusudama pieces.

Groom
Approximate finished size: 7" W x 16" H
Materials
Prepare [K]usudama pieces referring to pages 2-3.
  5 8" square tracing paper for coat [K]
17 5" square tracing paper for hair/sleeves/trousers [K]
12 4" square tracing paper for hair/collar/sleeves [K]
  2 2" styrofoam balls for head/shoes
  2 14"L #16 wrapped wires, Glitter glue (lame)

Brief Instructions
● Make shoes by cutting styrofoam ball into halves. Push wires into shoes.
● Pierce trouser pieces one by one with the wire. Check heights of both trousers, and glue to secure.
● Make coat by inserting four 8" pieces into one 8" base evenly.
● Bind wires cross to secure, and insert into coat. Push toothpick into head, and attach to top of body.
● Using threaded needle join hair pieces, and glue onto head.
● Join sleeve and shoulder pieces. Glue them onto neckline.
● Fill gaps between shoulders with 2 kusudama pieces on each front and back.
● Apply glitter glue as needed.

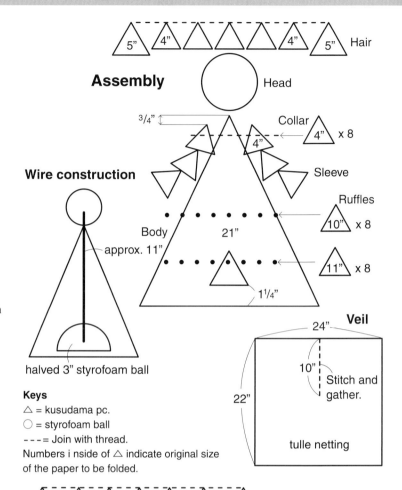

Keys
△ = kusudama pc.
○ = styrofoam ball
- - - = Join with thread.
Numbers inside of △ indicate original size of the paper to be folded.

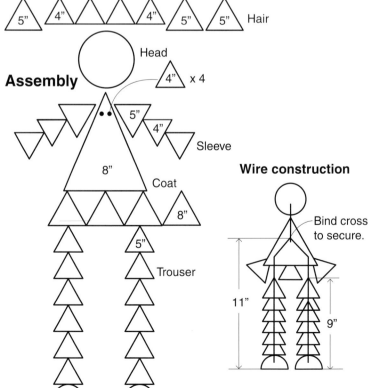

43. Chinese Dynasty on page 82

Collar
Fold origami strip in half.

Trim away.

fold — Collar

LIFE SIZE PATTERN

Leave 1/8" fold uncut.

Keys
△ = kusudama pc.
○ = styrofoam ball
- - - = Join with thread.
Numbers inside of △ indicate original size of the paper to be folded.

Assembly

Head

← Collar

2"

3"

Sleeve

8"

Body

Approximate finished size: 3" W x 5" H

Materials per figure

Prepare [K]usudama pieces referring
2 2" solid color origami for sleeves [K]
2 3" square patterned paper for sleeves [K]
1 8" square patterned paper for body [K]
1 3/8" x 2" strip solid color origami for collar
1 1/2" x 3 1/2" crepe paper (black) for base hair
4" x 2" crepe paper, cut into halves for chignons (Doll B)
1 1/8" x 3" crepe paper for braids (Doll C)
1/8"-1/4" narrow strip patterned paper for hair
1 1" styrofoam ball for head
10"L #28 wrapped wire
1 3/8" pompon (red) for Doll A or C
Wooden toothpick, 2 seed beads (black) for eyes

Braids (for Doll C)

1 1/8"
1/4"
3"

Twist.

Braid.

Glue.

5/8" 1/8"

Wrap with spare origami

Chignon(for Doll B)

1"
4"

Roll up.

approx. 1/2"

Fold into quarters.

chignon

2" 1/8"

patterned paper

Wrap around chignon.

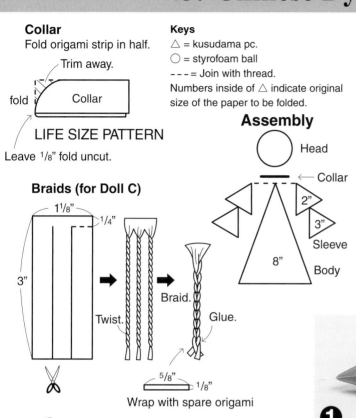

❶ Make sleeves. Pierce tips of kusudama pieces, and insert wire.

❷ Pierce wire horizontally into body, 1/4" below the top, through to the other side. Attach the other sleeve pieces.

❸ Join ends of wire, twisting to secure. Trim away extra wire.

Make collar as illustrated, and join ends. Glue to top of body.

❹

❺ For base hair, push toothpick into head, and wrap half of head with crepe paper. Apply glue, and round off top using a toothpick.

❻ Wrap with strip of patterned paper. Glue on pompon. For Doll B, see Step ❽. For Doll C, make braids and glue at a slant.

❼ Apply glue onto top of body, and insert head.

❽ For Doll B, make chignons and glue onto both sides of head.

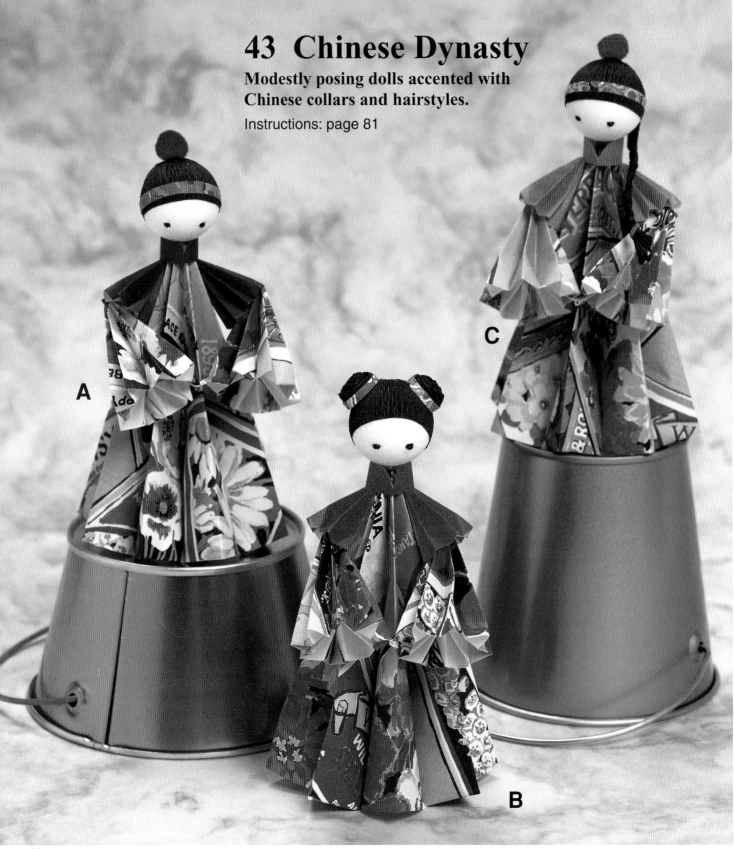

43 Chinese Dynasty

Modestly posing dolls accented with Chinese collars and hairstyles.

Instructions: page 81

A

B

C

Rear View

44 Vega and Altair

The legend of forbidden love seems to date back to B.C. 1 in China, when an epic was introduced: Vega and Altair had to work hard until their once-a-year rendezvous in the Milky Way. Today Japanese children make wishes on July 7 evening by hanging colorful notes on bamboo branches.

Instructions: page 84

Rear View

Vega

Approximate finished size: 4¹/₂" W x 8" H

Materials

Prepare [K]usudama pieces referring to pages 2-3.

1 12" square patterned washi for body [K]

8 3" origami (red) for ruffle/sleeves [K]

2 2" origami (pink) for sleeves [K]

2 2" origami (light pink) for sleeves [K]

³/₄" x 5" patterned washi for collar

³/₄" x 5" origami (white) for collar

³/₄" x 5" origami (light pink) for collar

1 1¹/₄" styrofoam ball for head

Fine pipe cleaners (black) for hair

1 ³/₈" star-shaped sequin (silver)

1 ⁵/₈" star-shaped sequin (gold)

20"L 1" organza ribbon, Bamboo skewer

Altair

Approx. finished size: 5¹/₂" W x 8" H

Materials

Prepare [K]usudama pieces referring to pages 2-3.

1 14" square patterned washi for body [K]

8 3" origami (dark blue) for ruffle/sleeves [K]

4 2" origami (blue) for sleeves [K]

³/₄" x 5" patterned washi for collar

³/₄" x 5" origami (dark blue) for collar

³/₄" x 5" origami (blue) for collar

³/₄" square origami (blue) for hair

1 1¹/₄" styrofoam ball for head

Fine pipe cleaners (black) for hair

Bamboo skewer

Brief Instructions

● Using threaded needle join 6 ruffle pieces in the round, and place on body.

● Make head as illustrated, and push in bamboo skewer. Insert it into body with glue.

● Stack 3 sleeve pieces each, and insert into shoulder ruffle.

● Make collar as illustrated, and wrap around neck.

● Put middle of organza ribbon on head and let remainders flow.

Collar (both)

5"

Fold in half.   ³/₄"

Slide ¹/₃₂" for each.

Layer 3 strips.

Fold back and glue.

Keys

△ = kusudama pc.   ○ = styrofoam ball

- - - = Join with thread.

Numbers inside of △ indicate original size of the paper to be folded.

Vega   Head

Ruffle

3"   3"

3"

2" Sleeve

12" Body

Assembly

Altair   Head

Ruffle

3"   3"

3"

2" Sleeve

14" Body

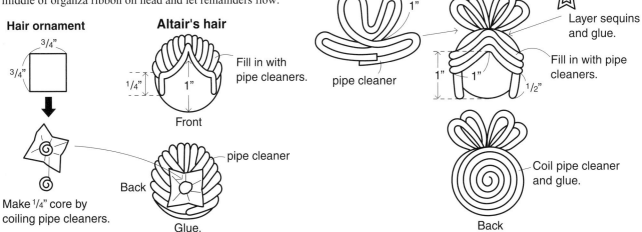

Hair ornament

³/₄"

³/₄"

Make ¹/₄" core by coiling pipe cleaners.

Altair's hair

Fill in with pipe cleaners.

¹/₄"   1"

Front

pipe cleaner

Back

Glue.

Vega's hair

Front

1"

pipe cleaner

Hair ornament

Layer sequins and glue.

Fill in with pipe cleaners.

1"   1"   ¹/₂"

Coil pipe cleaner and glue.

Back

45. Young Court Nobles on page 86

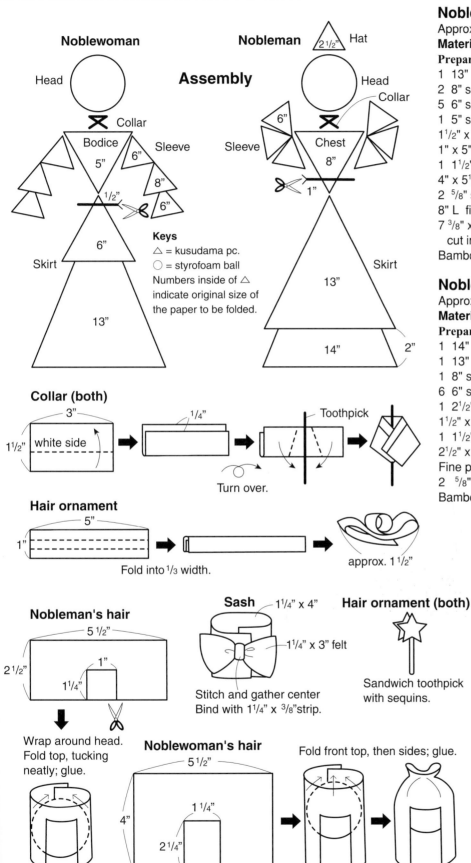

Noblewoman

Head

X Collar

Bodice 5"

Sleeve 6"

8"

6"

1/2"

Skirt 6"

13"

Keys
△ = kusudama pc.
○ = styrofoam ball
Numbers inside of △
indicate original size of
the paper to be folded.

Assembly

Nobleman Hat 2 1/2"

Head

Collar

6"

Sleeve X Chest 8"

1"

Skirt 13"

14" 2"

Collar (both)

3"

1 1/2" white side

1/4"

Toothpick

Turn over.

Hair ornament

5"

1"

Fold into 1/3 width.

approx. 1 1/2"

Nobleman's hair

5 1/2"

2 1/2"

1"

1 1/4"

Wrap around head.
Fold top, tucking
neatly; glue.

Sash

1 1/4" x 4"

1 1/4" x 3" felt

Stitch and gather center
Bind with 1 1/4" x 3/8"strip.

Hair ornament (both)

Sandwich toothpick
with sequins.

Noblewoman's hair

5 1/2"

4"

1 1/4"

2 1/4"

Fold front top, then sides; glue.

Noblewoman

Approximate finished size: 7 1/2" W x 12" H
Materials
Prepare [K]usudama pieces referring to pages 2-3.
1 13" square patterned washi for skirt [K]
2 8" square patterned washi for sleeves [K]
5 6" square patterned washi for sleeves/skirt [K]
1 5" square patterned washi for bodice [K]
1 1/2" x 3" patterned washi for collar
1" x 5" patterned washi for hair ornament
1 1 1/2" styrofoam ball for head
4" x 5 1/2" crepe paper (black) for hair
2 5/8" star-shaped sequins (gold)
8" L fine pipe cleaner (gold)
7 3/8" x 1 1/4" felt (red) for obi sash,
   cut into 4", 3" and 3/8"
Bamboo skewer, Wooden toothpick

Nobleman

Approximate finished size: 9" W x 14" H
Materials
Prepare [K]usudama pieces referring to pages 2-3.
1 14" square patterned washi for skirt [K]
1 13" square indigo washi for skirt [K]
1 8" square indigo washi for chest [K]
6 6" square patterned washi for sleeves [K]
1 2 1/2" square patterned washi for hat [K]
1 1/2" x 3" patterned washi for collar
1 1 1/2" styrofoam ball for head
2 1/2" x 5 1/2" crepe paper (black) for hair
Fine pipe cleaner (gold)
2 5/8" star-shaped sequins (gold)
Bamboo skewer, Wooden toothpick

Brief Instructions

● Insert lower skirt piece into upper one,
and glue to secure.
● To attach bodice on it, trim away skirt
top of noblewoman, chest end of nobleman.
● Make collar and head as illustrated. Push
bamboo skewer into head, and insert into
bodice through collar.
● Attach sleeves. For nobleman, glue 2
pieces onto valley fold of chest, and then
add another piece on top. For noblewoman,
glue 1 piece to bodice, and then add the
layered pieces behind it. Work both sides.
● Finish nobleman's head by attaching hat
and sequins. Attach pipe cleaner cut short,
pointing backwards.
● Finish noblewoman's head by attaching
ornament, and adding sequins behind it.
Make sash with felt as illustrated, and wrap
around waist. "Bind" sash with pipe
cleaner, and tie at front. Tuck ends under.
Glue on felt bow to back.

45 Young Court Nobles

Charming youths in lavish
costumes. Enjoy coordinating
solid color and pattern
in your own way.

Instructions: page 85

Side View

Rear View

46 Japanese Kimono Doll

Kimono with long, swishing sleeves called "furisode."
Young Japanese girls still wear furisode on festive occasions.

Instructions: page 87-88

Rear View

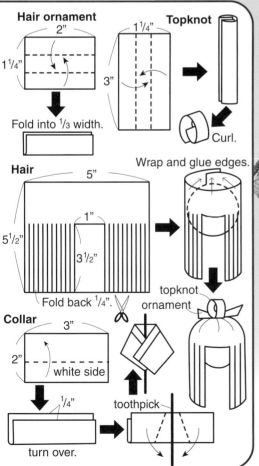

Hair ornament

2"

1 1/4"

Fold into 1/3 width.

Topknot

1 1/4"

3"

Curl.

Hair

5"

5 1/2"

1"

3 1/2"

Fold back 1/4".

Wrap and glue edges.

topknot
ornament

Collar

3"

2"

white side

1/4"

turn over.

toothpick

46. Japanese Kimono Doll on page 87

Approximate finished size: 9" W x 12" H

Materials
Prepare [K]usudama pieces referring to pages 2-3.
1 14" square patterned washi for skirt [K]
2 9" square patterned washi for sleeves [K]
2 8" square patterned washi for sleeves [K]
2 6" square patterned washi for skirt [K]
2" x 3" patterned washi for collar
4" x 12" solid color washi for obi sash
4" x 4" patterned washi for obi sash
2" x 5" solid color washi for obi sash
2" x 3" patterned washi for obi sash
2" x 1¼" patterned washi for hair ornament
1 1½" styrofoam ball for head
5" x 5½" crepe paper (black) for hair
1¼" x 3" crepe paper (black) for hair
2 6"L thick pipe cleaners in contrasting colors
Bamboo skewer

Keys
△ = kusudama pc.
○ = styrofoam ball
Numbers inside of △ indicate original size
of the paper to be folded.

Front obi sash
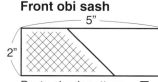
5"
2"
Paste check pattern
over solid, diagonally.

³⁄₈"
³⁄₈"
Warp around waist.

Assembly
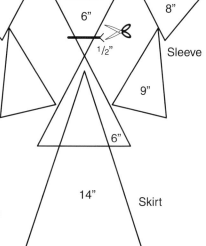
Head
Collar
Bodice
6"
8"
½"
Sleeve
9"
6"
14"
Skirt

Back tie of sash

12"
4"
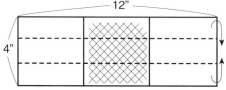
Do not overlap.
4"
Paste check pattern in middle.   Fold into ¹⁄₃ width.
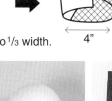

❶ Insert lower skirt into upper piece aligning pleats. Apply glue to inside of valley folds and stick to secure.

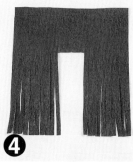
❷ Trim away pointed end of bodice, and stack over skirt.

❸ Make head. Push bamboo skewer into styrofoam ball. Wrap skewer with collar (page 87.) Glue ends of collar, and set collar aside.

❹ Make hair (page 87) using sharp scissors.

❺ Apply a line of glue around middle of head. Wrap it with hair without pulling paper.

❻ Apply glue inside thinly.

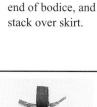
❼ Rolling a round stick or toothpick, gather top of hair.

❽ Glue on topknot and ornament (page 87.)

❾ Insert head into body, together with the joined collar.

❿ Glue on front obi sash, and attach back tie.

⓫

Glue gun
Use glue gun for small spaces.

Attach sleeves, 1 piece to each side, and to its back, glue on larger piece at a slant.

88

Empress
Approximate finished size: 4" W x 5" H
Materials
Prepare [K]usudama pieces referring to pages 2-3.
1 6" square patterned washi for skirt [K]
2 4" square patterned washi for sleeves [K]
6 3" square patterned washi for sleeves/bodice/skirt [K]
3/8" x 1 1/2" patterned washi for hair ornament
1 1/4" x 1" patterned washi for hair ornament
3" x 6" patterned washi for skirt overlay
1 1/4" x 2" patterned washi for collar
1" x 3" solid color washi for obi sash
1/2" x 5" origami (gold) for tiara
1 1/2" x 5" origami (gold) for fan
1 1" styrofoam ball for head
Habutae shiny thread (black/pink)
3"L mizuhiki cords (pink/red)

Emperor
Approximate finished size: 3" W x 6" H
Materials
Prepare [K]usudama pieces referring to pages 2-3.
1 6" square patterned indigo washi for skirt [K]
2 4" square patterned indigo washi for sleeves [K]
4 3" square patterned indigo washi for sleeves/chest/skirt [K]
1 2" square indigo washi for hat [K]
1 1/4" x 2" patterned indigo washi for collar
1" x 3" patterned indigo washi for obi sash
1 1/4" x 2" indigo washi for scepter
1 1" styrofoam ball for head, Wooden toothpick
1 bunch Japanese silk embroidery floss (black)

Brief Instructions for Empress
● Stack 2 skirt pieces and glue to secure.
● Stack bodice piece over skirt. Make head as illustrated below, and push in toothpick. Insert it into bodice, and secure with glue at a position high enough to show collar.
● Wrap waist with obi sash. Make decorative overlay, wrap around sash, and tie cords at front.
● Attach top sleeve by gluing to valley fold of bodice. Add 2 more pieces under it, at a slant.
● Make tiara, and glue onto head. Bind hair, and attach curved ornament onto it.
● Make fan and glue onto ends of sleeves.

Brief Instructions for Emperor
● Assemble body in the same manner as Empress.
● Wrap waist with obi sash.
● Attach larger sleeves to sides of chest. Add another piece above it.
● Make hat and glue onto head. Glue scepter onto ends of sleeves.

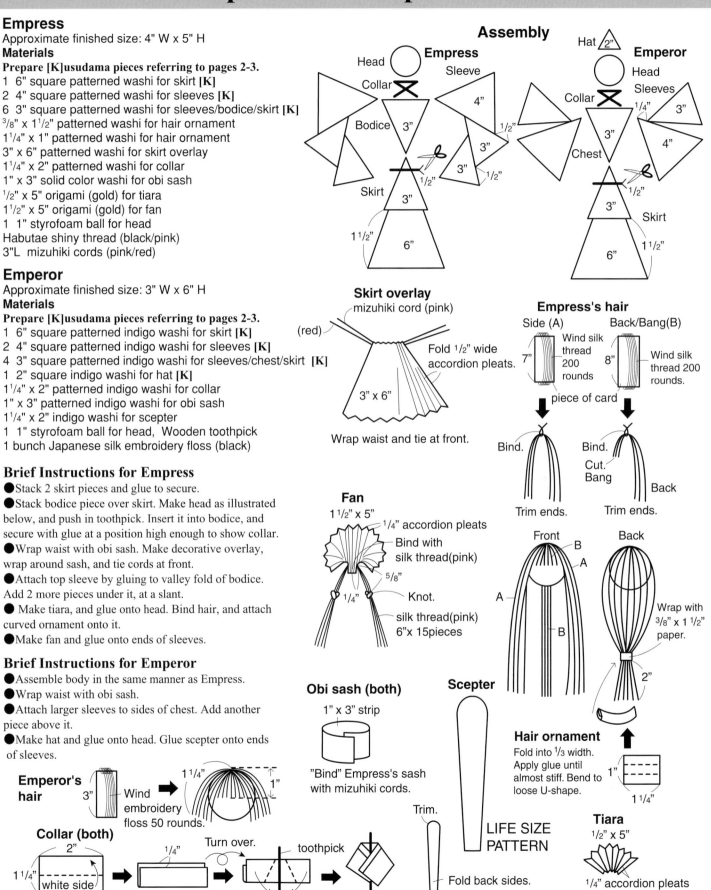

Assembly

Empress — Head, Collar, Bodice, Sleeve 4", 3", 3", 1/2", 1/2", Skirt 3", 1 1/2", 6"

Emperor — Hat 2", Head, Collar, Sleeves 1/4", 3", 4", Chest 3", 1/2", Skirt 3", 1 1/2", 6"

Skirt overlay
mizuhiki cord (pink)
(red)
Fold 1/2" wide accordion pleats.
3" x 6"
Wrap waist and tie at front.

Empress's hair
Side (A) — Wind silk thread 200 rounds 7"
Back/Bang(B) — Wind silk thread 200 rounds. 8"
piece of card
Bind.
Bind. Cut. Bang
Back
Trim ends.
Trim ends.

Fan
1 1/2" x 5"
1/4" accordion pleats
Bind with silk thread(pink)
5/8"
1/4"
Knot.
silk thread(pink)
6"x 15pieces

Front — B, A
Back
A
B
Wrap with 3/8" x 1 1/2" paper.
2"

Obi sash (both)
1" x 3" strip
"Bind" Empress's sash with mizuhiki cords.

Scepter
Trim.
Fold back sides.
LIFE SIZE PATTERN

Hair ornament
Fold into 1/3 width. Apply glue until almost stiff. Bend to loose U-shape.
1"
1 1/4"

Tiara
1/2" x 5"
1/4" accordion pleats

Emperor's hair
3"
Wind embroidery floss 50 rounds.
1 1/4"
1"

Collar (both)
2"
1 1/4"
white side
1/4"
Turn over.
toothpick

47 Emperor and Empress

The popular display for Doll Festival. Note the back with beautiful silk hair and overlay.

Instructions: page 89

Rear View

48 Sitting Emperor and Empress

A sitting version for Doll Festival. Lamps and topiary-like plants are made of kusudama pieces.

Instructions: pages 91-92

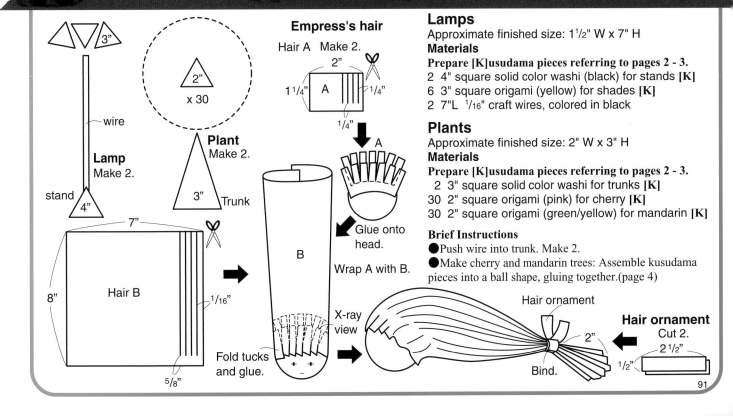

Lamp
Make 2.

wire

stand

4"

Plant
Make 2.

3" Trunk

x 30

2"

Empress's hair

Hair A Make 2.

2"

1 1/4"   A   1/4"

1/4"

A

Glue onto head.

Wrap A with B.

B

Hair B

7"

8"

1/16"

5/8"

Fold tucks and glue.

X-ray view

Hair ornament

Bind.

Hair ornament
Cut 2.
2 1/2"

2"

1/2"

Lamps
Approximate finished size: 1 1/2" W x 7" H
Materials
Prepare [K]usudama pieces referring to pages 2 - 3.
2 4" square solid color washi (black) for stands **[K]**
6 3" square origami (yellow) for shades **[K]**
2 7"L 1/16" craft wires, colored in black

Plants
Approximate finished size: 2" W x 3" H
Materials
Prepare [K]usudama pieces referring to pages 2 - 3.
2 3" square solid color washi for trunks **[K]**
30 2" square origami (pink) for cherry **[K]**
30 2" square origami (green/yellow) for mandarin **[K]**

Brief Instructions
● Push wire into trunk. Make 2.
● Make cherry and mandarin trees: Assemble kusudama pieces into a ball shape, gluing together.(page 4)

Empress

Approximate finished size: 8" W x 8" H

Materials

Prepare [K]usudama pieces referring to pages 2-3.

1 12" square patterned washi for body **[K]**
2 8" square patterned washi for sleeves **[K]**
2 6" square solid color washi for ruffles **[K]**
2 4" square solid color washi for ruffles **[K]**
8" x 7" washi (black) for hair A
2 1¼" x 2" washi (black) for hair B
2 ½" x 2½" solid color washi for hair ornament
1 1½" styrofoam ball for head
1 2" x 4" origami (gold) for fan
2" x 3" origami (yellow) for coronet
1 2mm seed bead (red) for mouth, 2 (black) for eyes
6½" L ¹⁄₁₆" craft wire

Emperor

Approximate finished size: 8" W x 9" H

Materials

Prepare [K]usudama pieces referring to pages 2-3.

1 12" square patterned washi for body **[K]**
2 8" square patterned washi for sleeves **[K]**
2 4" square patterned washi for ruffles **[K]**
2 4" origami (rainbow) for ruffles **[K]**
1 3" square washi (black) for hat **[K]**
¾" x 3" washi (black) for hair ornament
3" x 6" washi (black) for hair
½" x 2" origami (gold) for scepter
1 1½" styrofoam ball for head
1 2mm seed bead (red) for mouth, 2 (black) for eyes
4" L chunky knitting yarn (black) for hair
6½" L ¹⁄₁₆" craft wire

Brief Instructions

● Attach sleeves and ruffles (2 on front, 2 on back) to body with glue.
● Make head as illustrated. Push in craft wire, and insert end of wire into body. Secure with glue.
● For Emperor, attach kusudama hat and ornament. Glue on scepter.
● For Empress, attach coronet. Glue on fan.
● Attach bead eyes and mouth to finish.

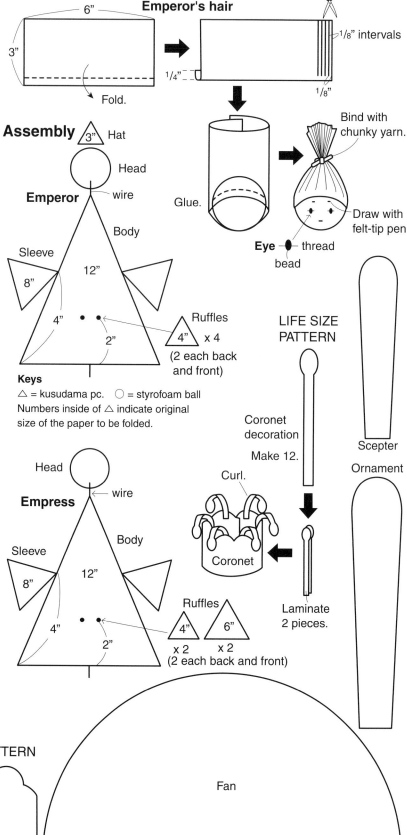

Emperor's hair

6"

3"

Fold.

¹⁄₈" intervals

¼"

¹⁄₈"

Glue.

Bind with chunky yarn.

Draw with felt-tip pen

Eye — thread
bead

Assembly

3" Hat

Head

Emperor

wire

Body

Sleeve

8"

12"

4"

2"

Ruffles

4" x 4

(2 each back and front)

Keys

△ = kusudama pc.   ○ = styrofoam ball
Numbers inside of △ indicate original
size of the paper to be folded.

Head

Empress

wire

Body

Sleeve

8"

12"

4"

2"

Ruffles

4" 6"

x 2 x 2

(2 each back and front)

LIFE SIZE PATTERN

Coronet decoration

Make 12.

Curl.

Coronet

Laminate 2 pieces.

Scepter

Ornament

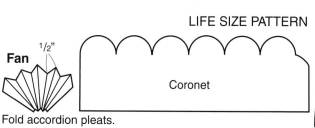

Fan

½"

LIFE SIZE PATTERN

Coronet

Fan

Fold accordion pleats.

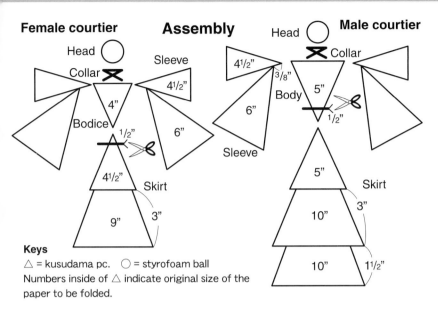

Female courtier

Head

Collar

Sleeve 4¹/₂"

4"

Bodice

½"

4¹/₂"

Skirt

9" 3"

Assembly

Head

Keys

△ = kusudama pc. ○ = styrofoam ball

Numbers inside of △ indicate original size of the paper to be folded.

Male courtier

Head

Collar

4¹/₂"

³/₈"

Body 5"

6"

½"

Sleeve

5"

10"

Skirt 3"

10" 1¹/₂"

Female courtier

Approximate finished size: 5" W x 9" H

Materials

Prepare [K]usudama pieces referring to pages 2-3.

1 9" square patterned washi for skirt [K]

3 4¹/₂" square patterned washi for skirt/sleeves [K]

2 6" square patterned washi for sleeves [K]

1 4" square patterned washi for bodice [K]

2¹/₂" x 3" patterned washi for collar

1¹/₄" x 1¹/₂" patterned washi for hair ornament

1¹/₂" x 4" felt (green) for obi sash (front)

1¹/₂" x 6" felt (green) for obi sash (back)

1 6" origami (red foil) for obi sash

4" x 5" crepe paper (black) for hair

1¹/₄" x 2" crepe paper (black) for topknot

1 1" styrofoam ball for head, Wooden toothpick

Male courtier

Approximate finished size: 6" W x 10" H

Materials

Prepare [K]usudama pieces referring to pages 2-3.

2 10" square solid color washi for skirt [K]

2 5" square solid color washi for skirt /body [K]

2 6 " square patterned washi for sleeves [K]

2 4¹/₂" square patterned washi for sleeves [K]

2¹/₂" x 3" patterned washi for collar

¹/₄" x 2" patterned washi for hair ornament

4" x 2¹/₂" crepe paper (black) for hair

1³/₄" x 2¹/₂" crepe paper (black) for topknot

1 1" styrofoam ball for head, Wooden toothpick

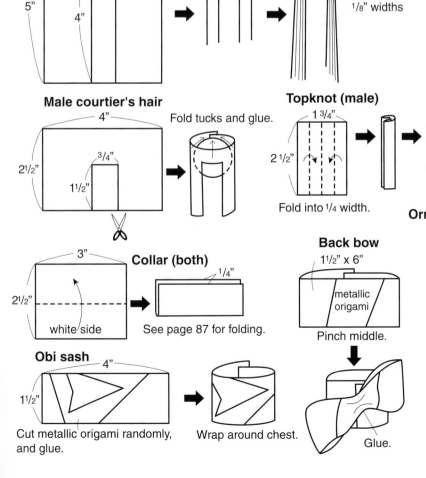

Female courtier's hair

4"

³/₄"

5"

4"

Hair ornament

¹/₄"

Cut into ¹/₈" widths

Male courtier's hair

4"

³/₄"

2¹/₂"

1¹/₂"

Fold tucks and glue.

Topknot (male)

1³/₄"

2 ¹/₂"

Fold into ¹/₄ width.

ornament

¹/₄"

Cut into ¹/₈" widths

Ornament (male)

¹/₄" x 2"

Topknot (female)

1¹/₄"

2"

Fold into ¹/₄ width.

Glue.

Ornament (female)

1¹/₂"

1¹/₄"

Fold into ¹/₄ width.

Apply glue and make a gentle U curve.

Collar (both)

3"

2¹/₂"

white side

¹/₄"

See page 87 for folding.

Obi sash

4"

1¹/₂"

Cut metallic origami randomly, and glue.

Wrap around chest.

Back bow

1¹/₂" x 6"

metallic origami

Pinch middle.

Glue.

Brief Instructions

● Stack 2 (3 for Male) pieces for skirt, and glue to secure.

● Stack on bodice. Make head as illustrated. Push toothpick into it, and insert into bodice. Glue to secure at a position high enough to show collar.

● For Empress, make obi sash as illustrated, and wrap around waist.

● Attach smaller sleeve pieces to sides with glue. Attach larger piece under each.

● Make collar as illustrated, and wrap around neck.

49 Young Courtiers

A "modern" version of Japanese dolls in semi formal outfits.
Enjoy free flowing hair.

Instructions: page 93

Rear View

50 Heian-Style Emperor and Empress

Luxurious robes that were typical of Heian period known for its unprecedented peace and stability.

Instructions: page 96

Close-up of Head

Empress

Approximate finished size: 9" W x 13" H

Materials

Prepare [K]usudama pieces referring to pages 2-3.

1 22" square solid color washi for skirt [K]
1 14" square tracing paper for body [K]
10" x 18" patterned washi for outer robe
8" x 10" solid color washi for inner robe
4" square patterned washi for fan
$3^1/4$" x 4" washi (black) for hair
$1^1/2$" x 2" washi(black) for hair
1 $1^1/2$" styrofoam ball for head
Chemical lace motifs, Gold thread,
   and Mizuhiki cord (gold) for coronet

Emperor

Approximate finished size: 14" W x 14" H

Materials

Prepare [K]usudama pieces referring to pages 2-3.

1 22" square solid color washi for skirt [K]
1 14" square tracing paper for body [K]
2" x 6" patterned washi for outer collar
1" x 6" solid color washi for inner collar
14" x 24" patterned washi for outer robe
6" x 14" solid color washi for inner sleeves
$2^1/2$" x 4" washi (black) for hair
$1^1/2$" x 2" washi (black) for hair
1 $1^1/2$" styrofoam ball for head
1 $^3/4$" styrofoam ball cut in half for crown
5" x 3" washi (black) for crown
Mizuhiki cords: 7" L (red), 16"L (silver)
8" L 1" ribbon (silver), Bamboo skewer

Brief Instructions

●Stack 2 body pieces. Glue, allowing $^1/2$" below the top of bodice for Empress, $1^1/2$" below for Emperor.

●For Emperor, attach collar and robe before inserting head. Wrap lower part of back and front robe with mizuhiki cord, folding horizontally. Fold silver ribbon and tuck in mizuhiki to hang at front.

●For Empress, make and insert head before putting robe. Make coronet with cut-out lace motifs, gold tinsel and red mizuhiki cord. Glue it onto head.

Keys

△ = kusudama pc.
○ = styrofoam ball
Numbers inside of △ indicate original size of the paper to be folded.

Assembly

Emperor's collar

Emperor's robe

Empress's robe

Fan Cut away $^2/5$ and center.

Emperor's Crown

Emperor's robe

Head (both) Cut darts and glue.

$2^1/2$" for Emperor
$3^1/4$" for Empress